*Researching, Writing, and Publishing
Local History*

Researching, Writing, and Publishing Local History

By Thomas E. Felt

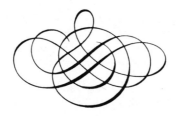

AMERICAN ASSOCIATION FOR STATE AND LOCAL HISTORY

Nashville, Tennessee

Library of Congress Cataloging in Publication Data

Felt, Thomas Edward.
  Researching, writing, and publishing local history.

  Bibliography: p.
  Includes index.
  1. Local history. 2. Historical research.
I. American Association for State and Local History.
II. Title.
D13.F387 1981   808'.0669021   81-10935
ISBN 0-910050-53-8   AACR2

First Edition 1976
Second Printing 1978
Second Edition 1981
Second Printing, Second Edition, 1983

Contents

Three Publishing   109

Foreword

Despite major advances in recent years in methods of communication, the backbone of the study of history is still the printed page. Television and radio, motion pictures and slide shows, audio tapes and museum exhibits all are means of gaining knowledge of one's community, but the starting point for those who develop media programs is most often the books and magazine articles in the historical society or public library.

The production of history in printed form is, next to collecting, the most traditional of all historical society functions. Indeed, it may be argued that collecting is itself the handmaiden of the research that is the bedrock for historical studies. Be that as it may, there is scarcely a historical organization that has not produced, or will not some day undertake to prepare, a printed history of the community it serves. It is for those societies, and for the persons who will do the research and writing, that this book is intended.

Research, writing, and publication of local history present special problems. The historical profession has many volumes on the general problems of research writing, but almost all of them approach history from a national perspective. For many years the standard and only comprehensive treatment of the subject was a publication of the Social Science Research Council called *Local History, How to Gather It, Write It, and Publish it.* Written by Donald Dean Parker, it was edited and revised both by a committee of distinguished historians under the chairmanship of the late Roy F. Nichols, and by Bertha E. Josephson, a member of the editorial board of the American Association for State and Local History.

The effectiveness of this collective effort is attested by the fact that it remained the standard for three decades. But before the book went out of print in 1974 it had become apparent that local historians needed a new treatment of the subject—something that would reflect the important advances that have taken place in recordkeeping, research tools, and printing technology. The Association took the lead in planning for a new volume and began the search for an author who was at home with the county records of the West and town records of the East, commanded the respect both of academic historians and enthusiastic amateurs, knew not only research and writing skills but also understood the special requirements of editing and publishing, and finally was able to write about these matters in a clear and readable way.

Our selection was Thomas E. Felt, a native of Florida, whose higher education was in Wooster, Ohio, New York City, and East Lansing, Michigan, and who has subsequently taught at the College of Wooster, worked for the U.S. Office of Education, and served as field representative of the Ohio Historical Society and the Illinois State Historical Library. In his present position as Senior Historian in the New York State Education Department, he works with numerous local historians, he writes, designs, and edits many of the publications of the State Bicentennial Commission, and spends much of his time dealing with printers and authors.

Perhaps best of all, Tom Felt regards history as something that should be enjoyable as well as scholarly. His wry humor reminds us that we shouldn't take ourselves as seriously as we do our serious work; and his zest for discovery and enthusiasm for his work should be a stimulus to local historians everywhere to work better, and harder, at the task of doing local history.

William T. Alderson
Director

ACKNOWLEDGMENTS

Louis L. Tucker first suggested that I might undertake to write this book in 1970, but neither he nor William T. Alderson and Holman J. Swinney, who were both extremely helpful and patient editors, could have known it would take so long. My greatest debt is to them. My thanks also go to Robert Richmond for his thoughtful reading of the draft, to my colleagues at the Office of State History—especially William Polf, Ruth Hewitt, and Bruce Dearstyne—to Adele Jackel and others of the Manuscripts and History Section of the New York State Library, and to Joel Buckwald and his colleagues at the National Archives and Records Center.

In spite of such generous help, errors and defects doubtless remain. Readers are invited to call my attention to them c/o the State Education Department, Albany, New York 12230.

T. E. F.

For this second edition, my thanks go especially to the good people who bought the first edition. Although more conscious now than I was six years ago of the book's limitations, even as corrected and brought up to date, I have agreed with the publisher that the best way to expand on matters too briefly introduced here is for the reader to move on to other books. As before, the bibliography (revised) is an integral part of what I have tried to offer in these pages.

May 1981   T. E. F.

Introduction

THIS book is directed to anyone who has already admitted an interest in studying the past and is now considering doing something about it besides reading the works of other historians. Reading histories is an essential part of the historian's education, but only a part. Mere reading also yields only a fragment of the enjoyment to be found in trying to comprehend something about the past. I hesitate to call the other part *making history*, or *creating* it, so for a lack of a more exact verb I will call it *doing* history. This is history as an activity, and it is what this book is about.

Local history is the book's special focus for a reason that is entirely practical. Most of the research and writing in American history for some years now has been on topics which are distinctly localized in subject matter and source materials. Yet none of the many books directed to the historian-in-the-making over the last several decades has been addressed primarily to the local historian. Now, for better or worse, one is.

Beyond the introductory discussion immediately below, the chapters are arranged to follow the sequence of the historian's work from first curiosity to first edition. Readers who have already substantially completed research on a project and feel ready to begin writing will find chapter II their logical starting place. Similarly, those with a completed manuscript will want to use chapter III first and leave the remainder for future reference.

At whatever stage your own work is in now, it will give you personal satisfaction only if it represents the best work you can do at the time. Measuring human expectations is always difficult and never final, yet it is continually attempted. When the subject to be measured is the working historian, two standards are essential no matter how difficult the application may be. One has to do with ethics and the other with competence.

There is an ethical principle common to all good work in history, whether the work be collecting, analyzing, editing, or writing history. It is not just the principle of respect for the truth, but of respect for the whole truth. The distinction is real. It is not enough to avoid lies; the truths that are told must be as complete as the teller can make them. This does not mean he should delay his report until he knows everything, or complicate his report until confusion leads to boredom and no conclusion is clear. In practical terms, respect for the whole truth means making an honest appraisal of all the facts and interpretations one has found up to the moment.

It must be emphasized that this is still an ethical ideal, and not merely a bit of practical advice. It is true that, whether he is labeling a museum exhibit or writing a biography, the historian who lets himself be carried away by the hope that he is describing a "first," "oldest," "largest," or whatever, may be in for some embarrassment. But there is nothing especially ethical about a desire to avoid embarrassment; even burglars take care to avoid discovery. Embarrassment is not the penalty to be feared. The historian who knowingly lets the truth be covered up or stretched out of shape may never be contradicted. His authority may be accepted in good faith. Those who doubt him may shrug their shoulders and say nothing, not wishing to upset him with inconvenient facts or arguments. The ethics of the historian are important precisely because he can so often expect his sins to go unexposed. This is even truer of the local amateur historian than of the professional academic. The latter usually has several experts in his own specialty who will read every word he writes and then publish their appraisals in the book review sections of the academic journals.

Sentimentality, poetic nostalgia, pride, whimsy, and wishful thinking all have their place, and a place should be kept for them. But not in history—not unless they are labeled and treated as what they are. They are the stuff of legends, poems,

CHAPTER ONE

Researching

RESEARCH is the process of trying to make sure that you know what you are saying is correct. You may write as fluently and publish as handsomely as the best, but weaknesses in research have ways of resisting every treatment except one, which is better research. *Better* does not always mean *more;* it does always mean alert, intelligent compilation and analysis of fact. Historical scholarship is a quality, not a quantity.

Some First Questions

Much of what an individual researcher in history needs will vary according to his special purpose. For that reason the discussion of a variety of sources and places is given later in this chapter in a series of short sections to be taken as needed, cafeteria style. But there are several questions that should be of interest to every local historian as well as to their colleagues in neighboring fields. I have limited myself here to three: (1) how does one choose between conflicting statements in different sources; (2) how does one really prove that something happened the way the best evidence indicates it happened; and (3) how does one deal with the problem of what motivates people to act as they do, and more generally, what *causes* the events we describe to occur?

I would like to take a slow (but scenic) route toward some answers to the first two questions by way of some preliminary observations on the relationship between historical and scientific studies. It seems worthwhile to do so because the idea of *proof* is basic to understanding what is possible and what isn't. (Perhaps equally important, it is basic to *accepting* what is possible.)

Historians cannot prove anything the way a mathematician can prove a theorem. There is a sharp difference between the mathematical proof, which is final and unarguable within the abstract world of mathematical symbols, and any other kinds of proof, including the legal kind. The mathematician can provide a perfect answer to a problem, but the answer may be meaningless or unimportant in the real world because the problem itself may have little or no connection with the real world. The historian is not free to go abstract by assuming that he has all the relevant facts (the *givens* in math) when in reality he does not. And on questions of importance to the historian, he does not. His facts are too thoroughly complicated by the variability of the human motives. Consequently, the best he can usually do with deductive logic is to *disprove* that something could have happened. This is important in preventing errors, but by itself it doesn't get the story told.

Here is a simple deductive exercise involving three quantities: $A = B$, and C is smaller than B. If asked how C measures up against A, we can safely say that it is smaller. This is fine as far as it goes, but not often useful to the historian because he rarely has problems involving just the sizes of things that can be measured. Note, by the way, that for A and B to be only approximately equal is not good enough: If A is 1,000 and B is 1,010, then C could be 1,009 (smaller than B) and still be larger than A.

The primary reasoning method used by scientists for dealing with the natural world is inductive logic. It is essential to the historian's approach as well, but it does not yield *proof*. Inductive reasoning gives a clear idea of the highest probabilities that can be found at a given time. Induction begins not with premises ("$A = B$," etc.) but with observed cases. The A is measured wherever it can be found, and so are B and C. If after the first fifty cases of each, A has always come up the same as B as a size of 1,000, and C has regularly been 856, then there is a high probability that future measurements will be the same. Problems of the deductive sort may be set up with *A, B,* and *C* and other quantities. But the high–probability claim is justified only when twenty cases represents a large sample of the expected total possible occurrences. The scientist may not know how many cases there could be, and of course his measurement of those he has observed may be off. Better microscopes and telescopes, for example, have made differences in observations which have upset earlier theories (inductive conclusions) based on too few or too poorly measured cases. So while the scientist may be quite sure of what he has seen, his predictions of future events is based on probabilities just the same as if he were giving odds on next week's football game. He gambles on a conclusion that must be tentative.[1]

One reason the natural scientist has gained such prestige for his collective knowledge of the way the world works is very simple: he has traditionally tried to keep the materials and questions he deals with narrow, specific, and simple. The advantage of this is that it has reduced the number of complicating variables and raised the confidence level of his research findings. The disadvantages of such narrowness have become evident recently in some areas where scientific research has been applied on a large scale in the economy. The terms *by-product* and *side-effects* have become familiar signals in the daily press that something has been misapplied. The response to these signals within the scientific community is worth the historian's attention.

Perhaps the biggest story in science over the past fifteen years has been the rise of a radically different approach to the understanding of the natural world—an approach that tries to avoid overspecialization and the oversimplification that goes

---

1. This does not mean that scientists are always so precise or tentative in describing their findings to journalists, or that journalists convey to their readers all the fine points. Neither does it mean that scientists are necessarily different from others when speaking on matters outside their research speciality—on politics, for example.

with it. This is the study of ecological systems.[2] It should interest historians because it has a complexity and scope that makes it very much like history. It is still not equally complex because it is less concerned with human variables over long time periods, but it comes close. Both the historian and the ecologist, for example, could study the impact of one of TVA's large dams on the Tennessee River, the ecologist concentrating on the natural systems and the historian on the human community. Each could learn from the other, and should want to. Ecologists are in great demand as investigators and predictors for public policymakers, but they recognize their need for the historian's approach and outlook in many instances. There is also an interest among some historians in writing environmental history, although so far this has been largely the study of attitudes and ideas rather than something broader. Actually, historians have long taken account of environmental influences as they understood them. Many of our regional and state histories, studies of the westward movement and the frontier, of agriculture, and of urban and rural social problems, could be cited as examples. A great part of the work of professional geographers in this century has also shown an awareness of environmental relationships, but they have been limited, like the historians, by the absence of the help which natural scientists have just recently begun to give.

The purpose of this round-the-world digression has not been to confuse you, but to cheer you up in the face of the knowledge that you cannot finally prove which documents, if any, are giving you the truth you seek. All of us have to settle for the highest probabilities we can get, based on whatever observations, documents, and combinations of deductive and inductive reasoning we can muster. It does not make the problems any easier, but it may be some comfort to see that in doing so we are taking a scientific approach to fact-finding.

2. *Ecology* is not a new term or specialty, of course. As a branch of biology it has long been given a chapter in high school texts (usually at the end) in which the carbon cycle, bird camouflage, and plant succession might be discussed. What *is* new is the widespread realization that humans are also involved.

Given the same problems, Nobel Prize winners in physics would proceed the same way historians do.

Choices and Proofs

Back now to the question of whom to believe when sources disagree. All else being equal, preference must go to the source which best holds up under the following three criteria:

1. *Closeness.* The source closest to the event in time and space, if not an actual observer or participant.
2. *Competence.* The source most capable of understanding and describing a situation.
3. *Impartiality.* The source with the least to gain from distortion of the record. A source may lack impartiality either by reason of a willingness to allow omissions and additions deliberately, or by reason of emotional involvement in the event.

Thus the ideal source of evidence on an event is the highly competent and impartial observer of it. You knew that all the time. Unfortunately, very little of what we want to know from the past is available from such star witnesses; historical events too often occur too rapidly or over too wide an area, among too many distractions, and with too much emotional impact on those present. A look at the problems that go with each of the three criteria may help in applying them.

Closeness. Historians have so long valued the contemporary accounts of events and the original words of official documents that they have often called them *primary* sources, relegating everything else to the *secondary* category. The only problem is that this distinction oversimplifies the character of what we actually get in contemporary documents. They are nearly always a mixture of eyewitness and hearsay evidence. Courts of law make a sharp distinction between the two, and historians ignore the difference at their peril. Then too, the time lapse between an event and its recording is sometimes so great that *contemporary* is a misleading term and the eyewitness has long since lost his focus, if not his wits. For one example, wouldn't you rather have a participant's recollections of the great flood of 1913 in Dayton, Ohio, given to you in 1923 than 1973, assuming nothing more was available from 1913? So would I. Finally, the praise implied in the term *primary* tends to discount the frequent shortcomings of such documents when tested for competence and impartiality. The test of closeness remains valid; it needs only to be closely applied. "Were you there?" is still a good question to start with, but it must be followed by "How long ago?", "Doing what?", and "Who are you, anyway?"

Competence. Like the other two criteria, this is a common-sense rule we try to apply in everyday life. The only caution that may be in order is to distinguish between one specialized competence and another. A witness may be mature, intelligent, and articulate, but still not know what he is talking about on the matter at hand. The draftee is not an authority on his general's strategy; the missionary priest is not expected to be an authority on natural history; the banker is an unlikely authority on how to cook chitlins.

Impartiality. Happily for the historian, certain types of records are highly reliable because they were created quickly and competently by people who were motivated to make them accurate above all else. In general this is true of statistical records of a routine or public nature: weather, tides, ship arrivals and departures, athletic contests, election and population returns, stock and other commercial market prices, and others. Official agencies which gather and report data as their sole function are reliable even when they deal in sensitive areas, such as the Bureau of Labor Statistics and its cost-of-living indexes. However, agencies which depend on others to feed data to them for compilation cannot always control the accuracy of their reports, as in the case of the FBI's crime reports.

Everyone has his enthusiasms and his phobias; the question is whether they affect his testimony on a given point. Everyone has his vanity and his pride. How are they involved? The plain, unguarded candor that historians prize so highly is probably least often found in the documents addressed directly to them. Let a normally open and confident person understand that he is speaking into the microphone for posterity, that his words will go into the archives and be weighed by future generations of self-appointed Recording Angels, and what does he do? Too often he becomes cautious, trite, defensive, and evasive. He sounds very much like a politician in a tight spot. He feels his self-esteem, or that of his friends, is at stake. He may feel his grandchildren are listening. They must not be disappointed or confused. The result may be something more like a carefully posed and retouched studio portrait, when what the historian wants is a series of snapshots. Another analogy may be recalled by those who remember the long-running television show, *Candid Camera,* in which the whole premise was that people would react to novel situations differently in private or in familiar circumstances than if they knew they were being watched by millions of strangers—and that the difference is amusing. The difference is less amusing but the premise is equally valid when applied to official public documents issued in explanation of events and policies. The State Department, for example, knows it is "on camera" when it issues a White Paper, and its overriding purpose is not to help future historians untangle a complex story, but to make the State Department look good. We sense this easily enough in following current events; the only reminder called for is that this is nothing new. The Declaration of Independence is not the place to look for an impartial capsule history of imperial relations in the 1770s.

There is a way to get candid snapshots of past events and personalities, and in principle it is simple: read a document for information it was not intended to give. You use it to yield answers to your own questions rather than those it was created to answer. This is detective work, but there are elementary as well as advanced applications of it. Here are two very ordinary examples:

1. A local store's business records were intended to keep track of daily trading and meet certain legal require-

ments. When no longer needed for these purposes, they might be used for the historian's. They can tell him who kept accounts at the store and when and how well, about price trends and interest rates, about credit practices in the time and place covered, or about the career of a prominent merchant and citizen, and much more.

2. A surviving batch of letters and documents, all dealing with the settlement of an estate, has served its purpose and a hundred years have passed. The historian has new uses for the material to identify family members, property descriptions, valuations, and more.

The archeologist is constantly pressing new questions on mute artifacts and forcing them to yield information far beyond their original purposes. The historian who succeeds in getting the most from his much more plentiful and varied sources is able to see them as stubborn artifacts as well as direct messages.

Closeness, competence, and impartiality—all three criteria are needed. If one of the two sources you are comparing is not a contemporary record and the other one is, then there is no question as to closeness to the event. But the later writer (the secondary source) could be the more reliable of the two if he scores higher on competence and impartiality. The writer may have used other contemporary sources of greater reliability than yours to correct or expand the story. Or he may simply have unloaded his mind and language of a prejudice revealed in the original.

Where the argument is between two later historians, neither of them witnesses, then the ideal solution is always to search beyond both of them into the contemporary records both presumably used to some degree. "Where did you get that idea?" is the natural question to follow up on. If the matter in dispute is a major one for you, this is the only satisfactory response to the problem. But if you are unable to get to the contemporary sources, or you feel the matter is too trivial to justify the effort, then you will make a choice between your authorities on the basis of what you can learn about them and their work—in other words, their competence and impartiality. This also calls for some effort if you are not already familiar with the books and their authors. Whether you find in favor of the earlier or later author is of no consequence by itself; information is sometimes gained and sometimes lost with the passage of time. Whichever may have happened in the case before you is what you want to find out, but there is no short-cut.

Why Did He Do That?

There are those who contend that answers to questions of *why* individuals or groups behave as they do are beyond the grasp of historians, and therefore they should not reach for them. "Just the facts, please," as *Dragnet's* Sergeant Friday used to say to agitated suspects. Without question the historian's first obligation is to establish *what* happened as best he can. But even if I were to agree that this should be the end of it (which I don't), I could do nothing to prevent you and thousands of others from attempting to reach for the *why*. It is too much a part of the simple human curiosity about other human lives to be resisted entirely. And it is too close to the heart of what makes any narrative interesting. The only problem here is that there is very little I or anyone can do to help you be sure you are getting to the *whys* of your historical past. Every historian, like every other adult, has his own views and intuitions on human motives. Historians believe that a study of history—and especially a study of the raw contemporary sources—can enlarge and refine their insights to a degree. But this can happen only when the researcher's mind is opened by a curiosity to understand, rather than closed by a passion to prove.

One suggestion: whenever you feel newly inspired by a really comprehensive and beautifully simple theory of human motivation, ask yourself whether it applies to yourself and your next of kin. If it does, then you may well have an idea for interpreting the behavior of others like yourself and your next of kin. If it doesn't, then you might better keep it to yourself until you are sure you are not being taken in by a plausble excuse for keeping an old prejudice.

There is no evading a plain appeal to common sense, or to that sober intelligence which is commonly shared but not so commonly used when needed. There is not much choice except to try to account for human motives, although a book full of cautions could be written.

In fact a good one has been written: David H. Fischer's *Historians' Fallacies.* Yet if I felt that the resources of the amateur were really inadequate to the challenge of historical research and understanding, I would not be writing this book. We are on common ground as amateurs in understanding the world. One of the most sophisticated historians of our generation, Jack H. Hexter, concluded toward the end of his recent book on the nature of the historian's work:

Above all historians must not be careless of common sense. Carelessness is not taking care, not caring. Not taking care with common sense, not caring about it is not caring about the most important means they have for knowing and understanding the truth about the human past. But to be careless about understanding the human past is to be careless of most of what we can know about men. It is to fail to cherish one of God's greatest gifts to humanity—the capacity in many things, if we exercise it with care, to judge men justly and rightly, and to understand men humanly and humanely. Not to cherish those gifts is to deny other men their humanity and thereby to debase and destroy our own.[3]

Taking Notes and Copying Documents

Taking good notes is a matter of settling on a workable plan and then sticking to it. Many of the details of the system suggested here can be enlarged and improved upon as your own needs become clearer. Your notes are your personal

---

3. Jack H. Hexter, *The History Primer* (New York: Basic Books, 1971), p. 296.

tools; the important thing is that they work for you. If you are not satisfied that your present system is serving as well as it might, however, here is a short how-to-do-it lecture that may be helpful.

Get all of your notes on the same convenient size of paper or card. I chose 5- by 8-inch sheets of paper years ago and have been satisfied. The same size of card stock is available when I can't get the sheets, but pads of sheets are cheaper. I like the roominess of the 5 by 8 and am rarely crowded in trying to get all I need on one side. If you want to interfile sheets of 8½ by 11½ inch paper that have been xeroxed or photostated, they require only one fold and a little trimming around the edges. This is seldom needed, but is less of a problem with 5- by 8-inch notes than one would have interfiling with 4- by 6-inch cards or sheets. Otherwise 4 by 6 is an equally convenient size, especially if your handwriting is naturally on the small side. But 3 by 5 seems to me impractical for anything but bibliography cards.

Expansion wallets which tie closed with ribbons are made for all the sizes mentioned above, and they are ideal for portability. Office supply stores also carry filing boxes in cardboard and metal. If their prices seem exorbitant (and they are), look in a secondhand store. A few will still have wooden file drawers which can be very good. As a last resort, use an old shoe box.

Confine your notes to one side of a sheet. A second sheet may be clipped to it if a continuation is necessary. But turning over to use the back side is a habit to stay out of unless you want to lose things.

Copy out the source of your note *first,* and fully enough to be understood a year or two hence. By disciplining yourself to get the citation down first (page number and all), you avoid the eventual certainty that one day you will not get it down at all. What happens is this: you are busily copying a long but interesting quotation when you are invited to lunch. Being both hungry and gregarious, you hurriedly finish the quotation, leave it, and return full of lunch an hour later to start on the next note forgetting that your last one is an orphan from a page and source unknown.

Make a separate bibliographical note card on each source the first time you use it. This is also a good place to record the library call number, and perhaps even the library. I also try to hedge against losses by also giving the full source citation as I begin my first actual note from a source.

Leave space at the top of your note for an identifying or classifying heading which may be added later. Even if you write in a brief headline or label immediately, to show at a glance what the note is about, it is well to allow space above it for still another line which might be wanted when you reorganize your notes.

Stay alert to your needs for both quantity and accuracy of quotation. When you are thinking best you will probably be quoting your sources least and paraphrasing most. You will only quote when you decide it is necessary, and then you will do it accurately, with prominent quotation marks, with every comma in place, and with every word spelled exactly as in the original. When less alert you will probably quote more often, promising yourself to think about the meaning or necessity of it later. Beyond this point of fatigue you need a break, because the next step is the researcher's equivalent of falling asleep at the wheel. You begin quoting without being aware of it, and quoting inaccurately. It is said that one man once wrote an entire chapter in such a trance, only to discover later that it was someone else's chapter.

In this same connection, remember all the devices for showing omissions in quotations, quotes within quotes, italics, and so on. (See the section on quotation in the Writing chapter.) When a quoted passage extends in the original from one page to the next, the break may be shown by a bracketed pair of page numbers: [57/58]. Insert the numbers in the quotation at the page break so that later if only part is used you will know which page you used.

In copying older forms of letters and peculiar styles of abbreviation, decide how you will be treating these in their final printed form and adopt any modifications while taking notes.

If in doubt, it is best to get a facsimile copy and worry about such translations later. Never try to reproduce the old long *s* form which is found in eighteenth century and earlier writing. It looks like a modern *f* but isn't. Neither your typewriter nor the printer can handle it.

Use the mechanical labor-saving devices when they are really labor-saving for you. When traveling on a tight schedule and paying hotel bills, it can be economical to pay for the facsimile reproduction of more documents and pages of books than you would otherwise want. Notes can then be made at home under less pressure of time, and the facsimiles offer a check for accuracy later. To sit in St. Louis wondering whether a quotation hastily copied in Washington is accurate is to be avoided whenever possible.

A variety of portable copying devices are on the market, although they are designed to meet the needs of small office operations rather than researchers. None approach the speed, economy, and versatility of the heavy equipment used in commercial copy centers and many libraries. If you feel you should consider buying, however, consider the 3M Casual Compact copier. At the present it appears to be the only dry copier at under one hundred dollars capable of handling bound volumes as well as single sheets.

Microfilm, xerography, and photostat reproduction are usually available at libraries, if not from the staff then by arrangement with outside professionals. Xerox, Verifax, and Thermofax are among the good choices for copying printed texts in small quantities. Frequently such copiers are available with coin slots. Photostat or 35-mm photography should be used for all black-and-white illustrations and any written material that requires high-fidelity reproduction, either because it is difficult to decipher or because you expect to recopy the facsimile for publication. Microfilm is the economical choice for large quantities of copying for reference. If something is already on film, a roll of copy film is quite inexpensive. Whatever copying service you arrange, expect to be asked for payment with the order.

Finally, and returning to your own note sheets, do not hesitate to jot down ideas and messages to yourself as you go along—questions, hunches, organizing ideas, or whatever, so long as it deals with the business at hand. Sometimes an idea comes only once, and there is no point in waiting to put it down later when you know it will be safely preserved among your notes if it goes in right away.

Organizing Notes

The final organization of your notes is a task that can wait until after you have made a convincing outline of your writing project. Until then it is nevertheless important to do something just to prevent confusion. It is well to have a tentative outline that will serve the purpose. It is a good test of your early planning to see how well that first outline serves to organize your research notes. To take an extreme case, suppose your original plan called for a chapter on the Indians before the arrival of the white man in your area. A year later, after extensive research, you review and discover that you have only five short notes under this heading. Apparently your area was either avoided by the Indians or neglected by the archeologists. It is time to consider whether your material is sufficient for more than one paragraph, and to think about what chapter to put it in.

When in doubt about how to organize any given batch of notes, try chronology. Getting miscellaneous information down in proper time sequence is always a useful exercise for the historian, and the resulting organization usually permits easy retrieval of a note. If chronology seems to be a poor idea in a given situation, you can always set up a miscellaneous section in your note file and dump the problem notes in there for later review. If a note continues to resist your efforts to fit it into a pattern that is working well enough otherwise, you may have an irrelevant note.

Sorting and organizing notes is usually a job best left to those quiet spells at home between research expeditions. A section of your file may be labeled "unsorted notes" and worked on whenever it begins to grow too large. The sorting process itself can be taken as an opportunity to read and reflect on your notes rather than merely shuffle and label them.

Libraries and Librarians

I will assume that you are familiar with at least one library and know how to get the best from it. There are enough variations among them, however, to make it worthwhile to point out some of those which could prove puzzling on first acquaintance.

One peculiarity of some of the special collections in the major libraries is that you cannot get in to use them without some preliminaries. This applies to university libraries generally, to the manuscript divisions of the Library of Congress and many others, to the Print Division of New York Public Library, to the National Archives, and to many rare book collections. If you are a college student you may be asked for a letter of introduction from your professor. If you are doing research on your own, you will need some identification and explanation of purpose at least. In some places (notably the Manuscript Division of the Library of Congress) you will be asked for assurances that you have read the published books and articles on your topic. Often a printed list of house rules will be given to you as fair warning that you may not use a pen, take notes on top of manuscripts, eat, smoke, or chatter, and may not expect to leave without having your belongings searched. Library security against fools, slobs, and thieves is never excessive and usually minimal in view of the annual losses. So even if you feel the precautions are misguided or misapplied, be a sport about it and give the librarians credit for trying to be good custodians.

Whether you anticipate clearance problems or not, it can be to your advantage to write a letter ahead of your visit, introducing yourself, and explaining when you are coming and for what purpose. Research librarians appreciate having advance notice and may be able to set aside the material you need to start on when you arrive.

Library catalogs are all basically the same in purpose, but

there are variations in their structure. If you are accustomed to the Dewey Decimal system of classification, you will soon find that most large libraries have shifted to the Library of Congress system. A few specialized libraries use the old Cutter system. Each of them will locate your books equally well, and the grouping of books on the shelves is similar for each. As a user it is more important to recognize that there are wide variations among catalogs in the number of subject cards and *analytics* they contain. The one reliable regularity should be the author card, or main entry. Titles are almost as universally cataloged. But since one book may cover five or six subjects, and few libraries will make that many cards for it, the sections of any card catalog given to subject headings will seldom offer a complete listing of the library's holdings on each topic. Moreover, catalogers do occasionally err in their classifications; in any case they may phrase or limit their subject heading in such a way that you miss or misunderstand it at first.

Analytics, in the librarian's lingo, are catalog cards made for magazine articles, signed essays in anthologies, and similarly distinct sections of series or volumes. Only libraries with special collections administered by specialists are likely to have such cards in quantity, and they may be kept with the special collections rather than in the main catalog. As I am sure you know, a separate catalog is maintained for serials (including annual publications as well as newspapers and magazines), and usually others for maps, pictures, manuscripts, and published federal government documents.

It is important not to be limited by any one library's holdings if you are to follow your research leads conscientiously. The reference collection of a large library should be your first headquarters in the planning stages of any project. Here you should find enough bibliographies, guides, and indexes to yield a long list of titles and a fair notion of which ones you should start with. As your guide to the reference collections, use volume I of the *Harvard Guide to American History* in its new (1974) edition. Chapters 4 through 8 are especially useful. These cover bibliographies, state histories and documentary publications, guides to manuscript collections, series publications of historical societies, and more. In most states, the best single guide to recent publications in local history is the index to the quarterly journal devoted to the state's history, since book reviews and notices are indexed along with the journal's own articles. In a few states an annual survey of research in progress and recent publications is available, either in the journal or as a separate publication. Another good annual compilation for the years it covers is the American Historical Association's *Writings on American History*. There is an index volume to this for the years 1902–40, a gap in the annual series then until 1948, when it picks up and continues until (at the present writing) 1959. It covers both books and articles thoroughly and is well organized. There has also been since 1963 an excellent publication offering not just listings but abstracts of recent articles in periodicals on history. This is *America: History and Life*. Details on this and the others noted here will be found in the bibliography. Guides to general periodicals, newspapers, pictures, maps, and manuscripts are also listed there and will be discussed under their separate headings below.

Librarians themselves are an invaluable resource to a researcher if they are cultivated with tact and respect. They are usually quite willing to help with library problems and may have the time and background to help with difficult research questions. From my own brief experience on the serving side of manuscript and historical libraries, I would say that the most important rule to follow if you want to enlist and hold the attention of a librarian is this: don't tell a librarian what you already know about your subject, but ask intelligent questions about what you need to know. At times you will feel you must explain why you need to know something, but keep it brief. The minute you lose focus on your unanswered question and slip into a review of your accomplishments and discoveries, you must expect the librarian to slip into boredom. And librarians like to avoid bores almost as much as they do boors.

Newspapers

Nothing quite equals an old newspaper for recalling the imagination to a time long past. The daily or weekly survey of bygone excitements and advertisements balances the familiar and the remote in a way that writers of formal histories would like to achieve but seldom do. If you have not yet passed a few hours browsing through the files of an old newspaper, make an excuse to do it soon.

If the enjoyment of newspapers is easy, the intelligent use of them as historical sources is not. A superficial familiarity with them invites a carelessness in their use which is especially unfortunate because newspapers will always be a major source for the historian. Every American historian should know at least Frank Luther Mott's fine survey of *American Journalism* and read the histories of the press in the region he is interested in, or studies of the newspapers he is using. The observations below are no substitute for such reading, but they are offered as an introduction.

The first rule for understanding newspapers is to remember that publishing them has always been a business enterprise. The second rule is that the profits in the business rarely have come from sales or subscriptions, no matter how large. Sales cover some costs of production, but normally it is advertising that covers the rest and determines the profit margin. Even the very early and small papers were useful as means of promoting their publisher's job printing business; Benjamin Franklin himself recognized this as a good reason for a printer to start a newspaper. There are, of course, apparent exceptions in the subsidized presses of political parties and churches, but these are merely presold advertising outlets. The point is that newspapers are not businesses conducted solely with an eye to pleasing the subscriber. They do not wish to antagonize their readers, but they cannot prosper by gaining more subscribers while losing advertisers. The same is true for magazines, as those who recall the demise of *Life* and *The Saturday Evening Post* will realize. Thus as a reflection of community life and attitudes, newspapers tend to be limited by the tolerance of advertisers. The nature of their readership sets another limit: the very poor, the non-English speaking, and the illiterate are neither subscribers nor advertisers. They may be ignored or they may be pitied or scolded in the press, but they are seldom represented in any direct way.

Freedom of the press has been one of the most valued principles in the American tradition, and rightly so. It has been maintained primarily as a shield against political interference. Against the economic pressures of the business community, however, it has very little application. The newspaper is a part of the local business community.

Colonial American newspapers were small weekly productions set by hand in crowded pages of the good rag paper—which was the only kind produced at the time. Relatively little local news is to be found in them aside from death notices, shipping notices, and official government reports. Ordinary local news had usually spread by word of mouth before the weekly edition was out. The stalest foreign dispatches had more novelty among isolated colonials; this news, together with political commentary on the major issues, made up a large part of the text. There were advertisements, but they were disappointingly brief, repetitious, and general.

Not until the 1830s did a radical change appear, and then it spread out only gradually from New York City, where the penny daily was born. As a cheap paper hawked on the streets for cash, the penny daily aimed at a wider circulation and sought for the first time to pay close attention to local affairs. The increasing number of daily papers between 1790 and 1860 (from 8 to 387) meant that regular reporting staffs were needed to feed the presses. By the 1870s, the city editor had become a figure of only slightly lesser importance than the managing editor. In this same period the tide of immigration made a market for foreign language newspapers, led by 56 German papers in 1856. Labor unions, churches, and reform societies were also sponsoring their own presses for newspapers and magazines.

Beginning in Chicago in the 1860s, a new service to small papers eased their production and made their numbers multiply. This was the preparation of *ready-print* or *patent insides:* the preprinting of (usually) pages two and three of a four-page paper with undated ads and feature material. The subscribing local editor then had to set type for only the remaining two pages to complete the paper. Over 1,000 small-town weeklies were supplied with such standardized insides by 1872, prepared mainly in Chicago by A. N. Kellogg or one of his competitors, and the peak was yet to come. By the twentieth century, a more flexible technique for the same purpose came into wide use. Called *boiler plate,* it was a column of type or an engraving sent out first on thin metal plates (later asbestos, for casting in lead locally) and suitable for mounting type-high blocks in whatever quantity the editor needed. Its proper name is *stereotype*, and it served the short-handed local editor well. The historian who wants to discriminate material of local origin from such filler need only be alert to the technique. Boiler plate normally shows a slightly different typeface; there is always the peculiarity of a nationally advertised product, anonymous tale or joke, or a special irrelevancy to the news which gives it away.

Photographs were not seen in quantity outside of the largest city newspapers until the twentieth century. At first they appeared among the more common line drawings and wood engravings. The latter were sometimes captioned "from a photograph," which nevertheless meant that a hand process intervened. For that matter, photographs themselves were frequently retouched to give them the necessary contrast for reproduction through the coarse-screen halftone engravings newspapers used. Usually the cosmetic work was so hastily done that it is easily detected even in the better reproductions in rotogravure sections—which became common in the 1920s.[4]

4. A reminder to researchers planning to reproduce halftones from old newspapers and magazines: normally, a copy photograph should be made of the picture first. This eliminates the pattern of tiny dots which make up the grey areas of all published photographs and paintings. Any printer can then rescreen your copy picture as he

Accuracy in reporting nonpolitical news has never been as much of a problem as completeness of coverage. Errors of commission are easily caught by those with independent knowledge of the events, and editors know it. Whether a given report is played up, played down, or omitted entirely, however, is a matter for editorial judgment which the historian may approve or not. Typographical errors have been with us always, but are most common in the early editions of daily newspapers. Proofreaders usually caught the worst slips in time for late editions, if there were any.

Letters to the Editor columns may be useful occasionally for reports of local events or personal witnesses in response to recent news stories. But as samples of political or other partisan opinion in the community, such columns are worthless. Between the peculiarities of those who write letters for publication and the biases of those who edit them, they lose all validity as clues to public opinion.

Interviews and Oral History

There are writers and nonwriters. Wealthy nonwriters, if they wish, can hire ghost-writers. The less affluent may have just as much to tell but cannot afford to pay to get their story on record. Rich or poor, there are many individuals whose memoirs historians would find useful as testimony on just one or two events—or on no events at all in the usual sense of the word, but simply for their fund of experience in a way of life that is passing. Since many nonwriters are good talkers, an obvious way to get their story is to interview them. The results are not guaranteed to be worthwhile, but "nothing ventured, nothing gained." It is like picking up a new book, except more trouble and more exciting.

---

prepares it for reprinting, although some quality is lost in the process. If it is especially important not to lose any picture quality—the finer distinctions among grays —there are experts capable of rescreening directly from a halftone and getting improved results. Consult with your printer first, however, and expect to pay a premium, since the new screen must match the old one exactly. If it does not match, the resulting image may be worse, not better.

The choice of whom to interview will be inspired mainly by the nature of the topic under investigation. You need a person able to "speak a document" for your use, and you can anticipate somewhat the quality of the document in advance. Knowing the person is much like knowing an author. It is not enough that he or she was there. What was his capacity to understand and explain the event, and what has happened to him since to flavor or dull his recollection? Interviewees are frequently quite elderly, but in itself that means nothing. Neither does a difficulty in remembering quite recent events mean that memories of events long past are clouded; the brain is not that simple an organ.

If possible, arrange interviews for relatively late in the research process. Your improved preparation will help in getting useful results in the hour or two available for most interviews. You will be more comfortable if you arrive with sufficient background to establish your seriousness of purpose easily and to build a rapport with the person interviewed. An interview is not a quiz; it should and can be a pleasant experience for both parties. If it is also to be productive, it must grow out of preparations made by both well in advance. You can do your part, and after sketching the outlines of the topics you wish to cover with the interviewee when you make the appointment, you can hope he does his.

The actual conduct of the interview also needs some forethought. Willa K. Baum, in her excellent booklet, *Oral History for the Local Historical Society,* offers nineteen tips for interviewers, and all of them are useful. Perhaps the following six *don'ts* summarize the most important: don't ask more than one question at a time; don't start off with delicate or difficult questions; don't interrupt (but instead make a note to return to later); don't put words in the interviewee's mouth; don't talk too much yourself; and don't forget what time it is. But Mrs. Baum's advice is better presented in four pages of her book, and that is the place to look for really adequate coverage of this aspect of your preparation, especially if you plan to use a tape recorder.

If for any reason you are not able or willing to use a recording machine, you can still manage in most interview situations by adapting the technique of journalists. From my own experience I would recommend the following approach. Equip yourself with a pencil and a pad of paper on which you have made no more than five or six topical notes—perhaps single words—as reminders of what you are trying to cover. On starting the interview, set the pad and pencil aside, reaching for them only occasionally to jot down names and dates. Otherwise give your full attention to the person talking and depend on your memory to retain what you will need. Immediately after leaving the interview, or at least on the same day, sit down and write out a summary of what you have learned and want to keep. Try to preserve the key descriptive words you can recall, but avoid quotation marks unless you are sure of the language. Then give one typed copy to the interviewee with a note—it can double as your thank-you note—requesting whatever changes are necessary for it to have his approval. On its return, revise as needed and then return a copy with a note saying that unless you hear otherwise you will assume this is now an accurate report of the interview's content. You should then have your document in usable shape and the interviewee will have his receipt. In my own experience, the length of such a summary has never been more than 400 words, so the post-interview chores have not been a burden on either party. Keep in mind that there is considerable follow-up work even when a tape recorder is used, since you still need to select and summarize material from the tape for inclusion among your other notes. Checking back for a review of even verbatim quotations from a tape should be routine. Anyone can "misspeak himself" inadvertently.

Obviously there will be some interviews that should not be attempted under procedures that put a heavy burden on the memory. Genealogical data and map or picture interpretation depend on details which ought to be kept in sight throughout the interview. There is also much to be said for taking unobtrusive shorthand notes during an interview if you are able to do it yourself. But having a shorthand reporter in the room with you is inadvisable. Any strange third party to an interview is likely to be more distracting than a tape recorder.

Occasionally you may find that some of your interviewing has been done for you, and all you need to do is to make notes from an approved transcript or tape. It is this kind of service to researchers that is the objective of oral historians. The term *oral history* has come into use over the last generation to designate a new speciality within the profession. It is the systematic gathering by one historian of a series of taped interviews on a topic, and is designed to serve other scholars who may want some or all of the documentation for their individual research projects. Thus the immediate product of an oral history project is not one scholarly book on the subject investigated, but a series of related documents which may be used like any other documents as sources for historians. Whether a project has succeeded or not depends partly on how well the historian in charge has anticipated the interests of future historians. The effort to create such documents is important now more than ever, not only because it accommodates the nonwriter, but also because in this century of the telephone, rapid transportation, and infrequent personal communication in writing, more would be lost than ever before if we were not compensating by the use of new techniques.

Anyone working on a topic in recent history and thinking of undertaking interviewing could profit from membership in the Oral History Association, or at least following their publications. While relatively few of the pioneers in this field have consciously exploited its value to local history, there is a trend in this direction. William Lynwood Montell's *The Saga of Coe Ridge: A Study in Oral History*, could probably not have been written in any other way. Paul Bullock's *Watts: The Aftermath* was an attempt to follow up on a local story of national significance. *The Foxfire Book* and its two sequels are the work of a country schoolteacher and his students.

Despite the growth of oral history collections initiated by

others and offered to scholars, it is still unlikely that you will find much ready-made for you. If you have the opportunity to include interviewing among your research tools, by all means take it. It is not a magic weapon. As one experienced oral historian conceded, "We listen to a lot of bull." But, he added, "It takes a lot of bull to produce a filet mignon."

Personal Manuscripts

Even the most hardened veteran of losing battles with stubborn historical sources approaches a new collection of private papers with a tingle of happy anticipation. Surely here is the candor and insight of witnesses to the past speaking to one another. Here are those most intimate of written artifacts—the family letters, friendly letters, begging and buying and bragging letters, notes, memos, diaries, scrapbooks, sentimental keepsakes, and accidental leftovers from busy lives. The historian recalls those times when he has found such unguarded doors to the past, and hopes that each new collection will offer him another.

His hope is not illusory, for there are such revelations to be found, if not in one collection then perhaps in the next. The challenge to the researcher is to prepare himself to take full advantage of whatever he finds. There is no perfect way to do this; one must partly learn on the job and realize that first encounters with the private papers of an individual are exploratory. Names, places, and events often require patient reconstruction as clues appear hours or days after questions arise in research. The usual problem is not that any secrecy was intended, but that the rapport among familiar correspondents allowed an informality that can make puzzles for the outsider. The historian becomes less an outsider as he reads further.

Just plunging in, however, is not enough. There are advance preparations which will help prevent drowning. Reading all the available published works on the people, places, and events involved is essential. There will always be name searching, map consultation, and more reading as the need arises later. But an initial orientation to the story told in the manuscripts is nearly always possible.

Another kind of orientation has to do with the story behind the collection itself. Whether you find it in a library or in private hands, try to learn what you can about how it has survived and what else goes with it—or went with it but was thrown out, lost, or given to others. Sometimes the answers are difficult to get. But it is important to know what the selection process was. Here are some hypothetical examples of what could happen:

1. Mr. X, in his retirement years, collected old letters and documents on local history from fellow townsmen who knew of his interest. On his death his widow gave his collection to the local library. Notes and labels in his handwriting are sometimes the only clue to the identification of pieces.

2. At an estate sale, a footlocker filled with letters, diaries, scrapbooks, and schoolbooks is auctioned off. The purchaser keeps the locker and a few items from among the contents and donates the rest to the local historical society.

3. The widow of a prominent senator and judge sorts through his papers at his office and at home, gives some to her children, some to the historical society, and some to the incinerator. Then she dies.

4. An old diary and several photograph albums are donated to the library by family members who share little curiosity about history and are not sure what else might be in the attic or basement, both of which are due for cleaning out.

5. A small collection of family and business letters is donated with the explanation that this was what remained after a nephew had taken what he wanted. The nephew is a philatelist and knows the value of stampless covers.

Such examples are reminders that every sort of accident and design may intervene as the manuscripts we finally get to read sift down to our desks. To know the story in each case helps in evaluating what we have. Why are envelopes missing? Stamp collectors. Why are family letters missing? The family kept them, or burned them—or perhaps none were written during the period in question. Why is there so much from one period of years and nothing from before or after? Perhaps there was a fire, an unsearched attic, or someone's decision to keep the rest. Every case is different.

Of course you do not need to depend on what sifts down to your desk through the efforts and accidents of others. You can scout for manuscripts on your own, and I hope you will. It is an enterprise that brings several rewards. First, there is the game itself, which brings out the detective in us. There is also the added value to your research, obviously, and finally there is the satisfaction of having contributed something to the common stock of sources available to others in years to come.

Your enjoyment of the hunt will be increased along with your chances of success if you will take precautions against complicating it unnecessarily. This means not letting a selfish interest in ownership interfere with your game, and not allowing vague notions of monetary profits to stir the cupidity of your prospective donor. Keep it simple: if a collection is worth preserving, it is worth preserving in a public institution under professional care. The way to get it there is for the private owner to give it outright. With the consent of the institution, you can be its agent to the extent of urging that the gift be made. Questions that tend to complicate the matter should be left to the librarian or others representing the institution. Where local history is the main subject of interest, monetary value is usually nil. Stamps, books, prints, and similar material which may have some market value are usually negotiable separately, and in any case should be thought of in terms of a dealer's offer, not retail prices. Questions of tax deductions should also be referred first to a librarian and eventually to a lawyer. Whatever happens to ownership, try to keep your attention on your main objective, which is to study and make notes from the material for your own research use. For many owners, this is a wish easily granted, however uncertain they may be as to long-range decisions. If a loan is offered to you, be sure to offer a receipt describing what you are borrowing and when you will return it. You may be protecting yourself against a misunderstanding as well as assuring the owner of your responsibility. As a young man with an honest face, I once accepted the loan of a box full of manuscripts worth at least $5,000 to a dealer (who would have sold them for twice that within a month) if the owner had been concerned with their monetary value. Fortunately, she was not, and I was able to study them for several weeks in the comfort of my back porch. If I were to return to them today, I would have to ask for them at the Library of Congress, undergo an interview, sign some papers, and then read the manuscripts under the eye of an armed guard. This is proper enough, but not as comfortable as my back porch.

Locating manuscript collections in public institutions is remarkably easy today compared to fifteen or even ten years ago. Until 1961 there was no nationwide directory of major collections, and unpublished statewide or institutional guides were scattered unevenly and obscurely across the country. Philip M. Hamer's *Guide to Archives and Manuscripts in the United States* then brought together brief notations on the holdings of 1,300 depositories, identifying 7,600 individuals and 20,000 collections, including archival groups. The next push toward a centralized list followed in 1962 with the first volume of *The National Union Catalog of Manuscript Collections.* This is a continuing and multivolume catalog published by the Library of Congress. Still incomplete, it nevertheless contains good descriptions of 18,417 collections from 616 repositories, and thorough indexes. Each collection is a group of over 50 items, and no strictly governmental records are listed. For full citations of Hamer, the NUCMC, and others, see the bibliography.

Libraries do not normally have their manuscript collections

cataloged item by item, but by groups. One card may summarize the scope of a thousand pieces or more. This is no
reason to despair, since a detailed finding aid may be brought
to you on typed sheets after you inquire about the collection.
Whether you are dealing with such a guide or a catalog card,
there should be no special problems in decoding the information offered as long as you know the peculiar abbreviations in
common use. Here they are:

D	Document (any manuscript except a letter, although some-times brief notes are designated *N* and telegrams *Tel.*)
DS	Document signed (not necessarily by the writer, who may have been the signer's clerk.)
ADS	Autographed document signed (autograph meaning "self-written" by the person signing.)
TD	Typed document
TDS	Typed document signed
Df.	Draft
T.Df.	Typed draft
L	Letter
TL	Typed letter
LS	Letter signed (see DS above)
ALS	Autograph letter signed (see ADS above.)

Each of the above may also be found as a copy retained by
the writer, in which case the word *copy* should follow all references to it in catalog entries, research notes, and footnotes. A
copy in this sense might take any of one of several forms. In
the eighteenth century and earlier, it would be a handwritten
transcription, usually by a clerk, in a book kept for the purpose. During the nineteenth century, the letterpress copier
came into use. This was a wet process of obtaining a facsimile
of typed or penned letters on thin tissues which were then
assembled and indexed by secretaries in every well-kept office.
Carbon paper copies have dominated twentieth-century practice, although Xerox and similar office copies have supplemented the onionskin "flimsies" in the past few years.

Whatever form it takes, a retained copy cannot be guaranteed to represent exactly all that went to the recipient. Normally it is satisfactory, but the distinction should be kept. There is always the chance that the letter was in fact not sent, or was lost in the mails, or arrived with last-minute corrections and addenda. Modern office copiers frequently have the added disadvantage of being insensitive to blue. However thankful we must be for copies of any kind, since they are often all we have left, the fact remains that a manuscript—literally something "written by hand"—must be considered unique until proven otherwise.

This is as good a place as any to take up a few of the more common problems in identifying manuscripts. Questions of date, author, and recipient are perhaps the most common. Fortunately, they are not often difficult to answer, at least for practical purposes. Remember, though, that whatever you figure out for yourself must be shown in brackets in any footnote citations—and therefore in your research notes.

The simplest dating problem is the document that shows "July 26" but no year. At least it is simple if the document can be fitted into a sequence of others, whether they are fully dated or not. The more of a series you read, the more clues you can pick up from the contents. To be at all safe, keep reading until you have more than one clue. And interpret them with caution. For example, your writer may allude to his preference for Cleveland for President. But Grover Cleveland was a candidate three times, twice against the same Republican opponent. You have a worthwhile clue, but still not a final one. Perhaps a reference to a family event somewhere in the series will ring a bell.

If you have the date "Tues., July 26" in the same letter with Cleveland's candidacy, you can get out your *World Almanac, World Book Encyclopedia,* or other source of a perpetual calendar. It will tell you that July 26 was a Tuesday in 1892, and not in either 1888 or 1884.

If you have no date at all on the letter itself (and check the end as well as the top), do you have the envelope or cover with a postmark? Do you have the letter it answers, or one written in answer to it? If they are also undated, you may get at least the right year from "internal evidence"—that is, from knowing what they are writing about and when it occurred, as in the case of the Cleveland candidacy above. If you have to settle for a notation such as [1892?] or [summer 1892] you may be disappointed, but there is sometimes consolation in remembering that date-hunting is useful only for a purpose, and you may have come as close as your purpose requires this time.

It is not a bad idea to read everything dated from the first half of January with a little extra care. I once had to arrange the papers of a prominent insurance and banking executive who always commanded a most efficient secretary. After catching her leaving the old year on the new year's dates a few times, I became curious to find out what proportion of her January letters were going out misdated, and arrived at the figure of two percent. This is probably a minimum.

If you have occasion to read documents dating from before 1753, you will sooner or later find that there was a period of uncertainty or disagreement as to whether the days between January 1 and March 24 belonged to the old year or the new. Until late in the seventeenth century it was customary to start the new year on March 25, and for several generations afterward usage was mixed. Recognizing this, a date might be written as "March 3, 1721/22," for example. We would call it 1722, but the New Style, as it was called, became official in the British Empire only on September 3, 1752, which was proclaimed to be September 14. The intervening eleven dates were officially "lost." In other countries the shift from Old Style (Julian Calendar) to New Style (Gregorian Calendar) was made at different times between October 4/15, 1582 (much of Catholic Europe) and October 1/14, 1923 (Greece). If your research or curiosity requires details, consult Section 30 of the *Harvard Guide to American History*.

To whom was a document addressed? Letters and notes written more than sixty years ago may follow the old convention of naming the addressee at the end on the left rather than at the top as we do now in formal correspondence. And there is always hope as long as the cover or envelope is intact. Keep in mind, too, that occasionally drafts or finished letters were in fact never mailed.

When you come to an unsigned document, you may recognize it immediately by the handwriting—but remember the brackets when making your attribution. If a second effort is needed, handwriting and similar clues are still worth following. Choose a candidate for authorship, and try to obtain a sample of his or her known handwriting of a date close to those in similar materials. You do not need to be a professional to check for similarities of letter forms, slant, spacing, and size. Other clues are spelling, vocabulary, and diction. When dealing with a person of some wealth or position before the day of the typewriter, remember that you may be reading and comparing mostly the hand of a secretary. When you see an unusually neat hand composing the body of the letter, followed by a contrastingly sprawled or crabbed signature, it is a good guess that a clerk or secretary was helping out.

One final note on manuscripts and then I will be ready to suggest that you learn by doing. If you are reading material dating from before about 1820, you will find the wildest irregularities in spelling and capitalization especially. They are not signs of a defective education. They mean only that our early writers had no standard guides in such matters and therefore allowed themselves an individuality, even an occasional whimsy, that embarrassed nobody at the time. Early English dictionaries were scarce and incomplete—the first included only the hard words—and Noah Webster issued his first little effort in 1806, followed by a larger dictionary in 1826. (These, or reprinted facsimiles of them, are handy reference tools if you are working in the period intensively.) The public school system, with its adoption of such popular new schoolbooks as the McGuffey Readers and Spellers (1837 ff.) had not yet had its standardizing effect. If you want to make judgments on the educational levels of our early letter writers, there are ways. Vocabulary, sentence structure, and general coherence are all fair game, but not spelling. Our early ancestors cared no more for its regularity than Shakespeare did.

Pictures

Only some pictures are worth the proverbial thousand words; others may be worth a hundred or so if intelligently used. Some make so many puzzles they need a thousand words to give them any value at all. Yet we all want more pictures dealing with the subject of our research, and properly so. Experience has taught us from childhood the impact a vivid image can have—the suddenness of its appearance, unlike those images gathered word by word through speech or print. Textures, lights, spaces, sizes, moods, and gestures are sensed together and instantly before they may be studied separately in the scanning that follows. A truly evocative image makes an imprint on the viewer before his critical powers can start into operation, with the lasting result that for all of us certain pictures have an unexplained attraction or repulsion. Nevertheless, the historian welcomes the return of his critical faculties. If an image is more than a document for analysis, it is still a functioning picture. If a picture is more than the sum of its details, the details are still worth attention if they speak to the historian's needs.

Massive and well-organized collections of pictures may be found in many public institutions and as the holdings of private businesses which supply publishers and other commercial users. The guide to these sources is the book *Picture Sources,* listed in the bibliography.

But for the local historian, the obvious place to look for his best pictures is in the same places he looks for his other material. Pictures often come with personal manuscript collections, and may be kept with archival records. Family albums may skimp on readily identifiable pictures—but check the backs of them and, of course, with any living descendants you can find. The stock of an old or defunct professional photographer's shop may be a gold mine of local scenes and faces. Some individual collectors of local history are good sources of pictures, as are the historical societies and some long-lived local institutions—churches, fire departments, libraries, clubs, schools, and newspapers among them. Libraries and historical societies tend to be the beneficiaries of other peoples' unidentified curiosities. Understanding this, you will be quicker to help them interpret their holdings when you can, rather than blame them for their ignorance. "They don't know what they have" is a complaint frequently hurled at local societies in particular. Human frailty being still with us, the complaint is sometimes justified, but a helping hand from a patient researcher such as yourself is generally what is needed most.

Another possible source of pictures is yourself. That is, you may have photographs taken to illustrate how a scene has changed or not changed. This should be a simple assignment for anyone who knows his cameras and is not rushed. You might go with the photographer, however, to make sure he gets the angles you want, and to get the permissions of property owners whose privacy may be involved.

As you collect pictures, inevitably you handle them, mark them for identification, and store them. To the extent that you do, you are a curator. All visual documents of any age have this peculiarity: they are instantly destructible by merely ignorant handling, not to mention carelessness. One rule of thumb will keep you from causing most kinds of harm in the short run, but it deserves memorizing: do not let anything but clean paper touch either the front or back surfaces. No fingers, no pencils or pens, except at the outside margins. Whatever framing you find, leave intact if possible. If it is necessary to remove a picture from its frame in order to photograph it, make sure the owner or curator is present and willing. If identifications need to be made for a picture, use a separate piece of paper and tape it to one edge.

The long-term care of pictures is a subject beyond the scope of this book. As long as your custody is only temporary, the only cautions you need to observe are to avoid unnecessary exposure to light, heat, and dampness, and to keep them from contact with very cheap paper, such as newsprint, which contains some free acid.

Interpreting Pictures

Ideally, you will have it all handed to you: who made this picture, how, at what time, of which subject, located where. Realistically, you will have to reach for most of what you can learn even to an approximation. But fortunately, something can nearly always be learned with a little historical "sherlocking."

A picture is an object which deals with a subject. The reader of your history will above all expect you to help him see the picture's subject. Show him where or who and when the subject is. If you don't know exactly, tell what you can and admit the obscurity of the rest. If you know more than you expect your readers to care about, you can choose your emphasis, cut the captions short, and file the remainder until someone asks for more. Every picture is a unique problem of explanation, and there is no guidance to be found in a book such as this except whatever may be useful from a quite different approach.

The other approach is this: since a picture is also an object created by someone, to interpret it from this angle is equally essential if the reader is not to be misled. Put another way, a picture is the subject seen through a process of picture-making. And on historical picture-making there are books that can help. They may be divided according to the two largest categories of originals: freehand art and photography.

The media of freehand pictures include drawings (in pencil, charcoal, or ink, most commonly), prints (including etchings, engravings, mezzotints, lithographs, woodcuts, wood engravings, and more), and paintings (whether in oil, watercolor, or one of the modern synthetic media). The most difficult media to distinguish are those used in drawing and printmaking. In general, you will see more prints than original drawings. In order to avoid calling a lithograph an etching, consult a dealer or a knowledgeable collector if you cannot locate a copy of William N. Ivans's *How Prints Look*. Knowing the medium can help in identifying and dating a picture. For example, there is no lithography from the colonial and Revolutionary periods; the process was invented in Bavaria in 1798. Even when a given technique has been known for a long period, it has varied in popularity and application.

Knowing who the artist was simplifies other identification problems. A great many obscure names are included in the "who's who" directories on art in the college and research libraries. Even a work that is unsigned and undated need not be a total mystery. Stylistic traits can offer clues to one familiar with art history. The most difficult art to identify on style alone is that of the naïve painter whose lack of training puts him beyond the stylistic influences of his time.

Photography has a fascinating history, and any nineteenth-century photograph you need to interpret should be welcomed as an excuse to dip into the books by Robert Taft or Beaumont Newhall on the subject. There were no photographs before 1839, and very few before the Mexican War years. Even then they were not paper prints made from film. They were *daguerreotypes* (named after the French inventor, Louis J. M. Daguerre and pronounced "daguerre-o-type," not "daguerr-e-o-type"), delicate silvery images on metal mounted under glass. A variant called the *ambrotype* became popular in the 1850s, and by the time of the Civil War there were tintypes (on coated sheet iron) and photographs printed on paper, developed from glass negatives. For the remainder of the century the succession of styles is important to understand, as the art grew in commercial importance and aesthetic self-consciousness. Amateur photography received its first great encouragement in 1888 with the introduction of the Kodak camera with roll film. "You push the button and we do the rest," the ads said. Kodak snapshots from cameras produced between 1888 and 1897, incidentally, were 2½ inches across and round rather than rectangular. The film was not equally sensitive to all colors; this would be true of all black-and-white films used by amateurs through the 1930s. Reds became black, greens were dark, and blues were light. A red-head appeared as a brunette, and lipstick looked like tar. The early Kodak was the forerunner of the box camera called the Brownie: its shutter speed was fixed at about 1/25th of a second and its fixed focus lens made a blur of anything closer than ten feet. More sophisticated cameras were always available in the early Kodak years, but ironically, professionals often used them to achieve a soft focus on purpose.

In summary, it should be evident that pictures of every kind are anything but self-explanatory images of nature. As every photographer and artist knows, there is a degree of distortion in all pictures. That cannot be helped. It can be understood, however, not only as a limitation but also as a source of the expressive power images have always had.

Maps

Time and space are related not only in Einstein's theories, but in the everyday work of historians and geographers as well. The historian can make sense of mankind's wanderings over time only if he can also track his subject through space. *Space tracking* is the wrong term, but it gives the right idea of why the historian needs the typical product of the geographer's work—maps of landforms, water depths, vegetation, population, transportation, communication, and all the variations on all of these and more.

The earliest maps of a locality are usually sketch maps made by explorers and prospectors or military officers. Their accuracy is uneven. Just as with writing, mapmaking is always done with a special purpose. What is unknown or uninteresting to the maker is omitted, generalized, or guessed at. What the maker does know may be distorted by his wish to make a point, since maps have been used for propaganda as well as for enlightenment. But the bias of a mapmaker usually is no different or worse than that of a writer, and detecting it requires only the same alert curiosity about the people behind the product.

Today we have the resort developers' maps published in brochures and magazines as bait for restless romantics. In the nineteenth century there were examples of the same sort of wish-fulfilling maps designed to lure the hopeful and catch the down payment. Charles Dickens needled these perpetrators gleefully in *Martin Chuzzlewit.* Over the same century, however, a stock of government-sponsored surveys of high reliability was also accumulating, first in the Old Northwest Territory and then beyond the Mississippi along the proposed transcontinental railroad routes.

After the Civil War, the county atlases began to appear in quantity, and these are often the most accessible sources of old place names and property lines, especially in the midwestern states. From 1865 on, there is seldom a shortage of adequate maps of man's locations, divisions, and constructions even in the newly-settled regions of the country. Good topographic maps on a large scale were not plentiful until later. These came with the growth of the U.S. Geological Survey, and its earlier products are now historical maps at least in their notations of man-made features, and often even in the physical contours they describe.

For seeing the landforms as they exist today, nothing surpasses the 7½-minute quadrangle series from the U.S. Geological Survey. On a scale of 1:24,000, or 1 inch to 2,000 feet, they may be compared to a clear view from a high-flying airplane. They show not only individual buildings in rural areas, but forests, orchards, power lines, ponds, railroad tracks (including spurs, sidings, yards, and abandoned lines), creeks, river channels, quarries, bogs, highways, country roads, and dirt roads. They are inexpensive, and one fits neatly beside another when combined in a mosaic. At 22 by 27 inches per sheet, they may be fitted together on a wall or rolled or stored flat. I once had over thirty of them assembled on one wall of my office, and the effect was most impressive. Whether I would have tired of it eventually I never knew, since I was shortly assigned to another office and had to disassemble the whole creation.

Such *topo* maps may be bought at many sporting goods stores where hunters and hikers shop, or from the U.S. Geological Survey's Map Information Office, Washington, D.C. 20242. Ask first for a state index map, or find one at a library, in order to learn what is available and get the identifying names and numbers. Many of these 7½-minute sheets are now in revised editions, so you may want to look for the older versions in libraries or compare them with the older 15-minute quadrangle maps, scaled at 1:62,500. The latter cover an area four times larger on a 17- by 21-inch sheet, and may be more practical if you want to assemble an entire state.

In looking for maps, every library is an obvious checkpoint. As in the case of pictures, however, maps are often not cataloged, so personal inquiries are justified. Town and county offices are also rich sources of maps, for local officials need at least plat maps, highway, traffic, utility, and election district maps in their work. A professional surveyor should be a good guide to these and other possibilities.

Because so much can be explained on good maps, you may want to consider providing your own adaptations for your publication. The clarity you want for your readers may not be possible unless you offer the right scale and simplicity. If this means making your own map, there is no reason not to. You might start with a USGS topographical map as a base (they are not copyrighted), trace what you want from it, and then add the necessary special features on the tracing. Remember that the second color must be isolated on a transparent overlay before a two-color map is ready for the printer. And remember to indicate whether you have kept to scale. Count on going through the map-drawing exercise twice before publication— once on your own and again with a skilled draftsman to tidy up and supply the neat lettering. A surveyor or a commercial artist who can take over at the final stage should not be hard to find at a reasonable price.

If this line of advice on making your own map seems to jump a step ahead of the research process, I can only reply that as a practical matter it may be wise to think about such a jump while the sources are still at hand. What I have called "your own map" will be, if it is a good one, basically a type of quotation from one or more sources selected and combined in a new way. If you can appreciate the possibilities of some of the maps and data you come across in the research process before it is too late, you can plan your needs in an orderly way. It is too easy to assume in advance that we are going to explain our story in words alone, and then realize only belatedly that there are times when a map (or an illustration, for that matter) would be not just a decoration but a forceful and efficient means of communicating.

Organizational Records

For all their differences, government agencies, business firms, unions, and churches have one common trait: they are all large human organizations structured so as to get their work done with some efficiency. That is a roundabout way of saying they are bureaucracies. Whether they are actually efficient in operation is of little importance to the researcher at the outset. His first concern is to understand the records. The key to understanding them is to understand that they reflect the formal structure of the organizations themselves. You have to know something about how the machine was supposed to operate before you can judge how well it operated, and who really operated it, and what it accomplished at any given time. Fortunately, the general outlines are simple and the peculiarities of any given organization may be learned as you study its records or acquire an expert guide to them. Technical terms including job titles, shop slang, and abbreviations can be obstacles, but there is no royal road around them.

Of course you do not need to know everything in order to know something. Your curiosity about any given organization may be limited to one of its products. Perhaps the most common example of this is the federal census. A great many researchers use it as their authoritative source on certain statistical questions without ever asking how reliable it is. Some scholars have taken a closer look, examining the statutes defining the special traits of each decade's census and reading the critiques of them and of the Bureau's performance. Occasionally someone takes an interest in the history of the Census Bureau itself, and it is only then that a visit to the agency and the National Archives is required. On the local level and a different problem: if all you want is the record of retail food prices at a given time and place, you only need one kind of store record. If you want to know how profitable the store was or how it trained and treated its employees, you need many more kinds of records and much more patience.

But it is time to get down to specifics. As on other topics, I will try to point the way as far as seems worthwhile in a book intended to cover all localities, and then to suggest ways to investigate your special area more thoroughly.

State and Local Government Records

You may not know much about government, but your government has always known a lot about you and your ancestors. All the highlights and turns of fortune in life have long been recorded somewhere in the official records: birth, death, taxes, inheritances, licenses, marriage and divorce, property transfers, bankruptcies, and lawsuits. Success with the questions of researchers depends on what governments have recorded and are willing to *tell*. Some records are always missing, and a few are not open to researchers for good reasons, but usually enough remain to make the search worthwhile for individual cases and to give a reasonably complete picture of well-defined groups.

Government archives are not for browsers.[5] Even if it were allowed it would be no fun. Official records are seldom entertaining and often dusty. Their investigation is only worth pur-

5. The term *archives* is used here in the conventional American sense of a depository of unpublished official records considered to have lasting value. It is also proper to speak of business archives, church archives, and the like, but I have used the term *organizational* records to cover the broadest number of similar types.

suing when you have some clearly defined historical questions in mind and some idea of what records should yield the answers.

Perhaps you want to know who owned the land along a certain stretch of river now located in one county, and to whom they sold it and when and for how much. This line of questioning is so similar to that of the land title searchers' that a sensible plan would be to approach your county clerk (in most localities) and proceed as if it were a title search. Or perhaps you want to learn who the village council members were and what they were up to in the 1870s. You should be able to trace them through the office of the village clerk or its successor. But be prepared to guess wrong now and then. Old local records are sometimes relegated to those who are willing to house them whether they are entitled to them or not. And keep in mind that certain records are in more than one place, at least at the beginning. In some states, duplicates of birth and death records, for example, are kept by a state agency.

If you are working on strange territory outside your own state, it is helpful to know something about the several main patterns of local government across the country. Every state is divided into counties except Louisiana, which calls its comparable units parishes. The only subdivisions not included in counties are certain large cities in a few states. In these cases the cities have been given county functions, usually only in the twentieth century. The most extreme case is Virginia, which has 96 counties and 38 independent cities. New York has 57 counties and the five boroughs of New York City, each borough doubling as a county. San Francisco, Denver, Honolulu, and St. Louis also double as counties.

The next complication is that the common terms in local government have no standard definitions. In the New England states, the unit with most local authority is the town. (The extreme cases are Connecticut and Rhode Island, where counties are merely court jurisdictions.) But the term *town* in New England, and in New York as well, does not mean an urban center comparable to a village or city. It means a subdivision of a county similar to the township in the midwest, but with more important functions. Thus in these northeastern states, all farmers live in towns even though they live in the country.

In the southeast, where early settlement was more often rural, the county has always been the major subdivision. Townships exist as unimportant units within counties. The Middle Atlantic states vary between these extremes, and as the newer states to the west were organized they created townships in the rural areas, but incorporated separately from them as towns those urban settlements larger than villages but smaller than cities. To confuse matters further, *township* was also the term used for the land surveyor's unit of six miles square. It may or may not represent the bounds of a political subdivision by the same name.

In all, there are around 81,000 units of local government with assorted names, duties, and structures in the fifty states. Not all of them keep their own records permanently, or keep records historians are likely to need. The most reliable clues for the researcher must be based on practices within a given state. With that caution, here is a list of strong possibilities based on the more common practices.

Land transactions: Recorder of Deeds (county), County Clerk, Town Clerk (New England).

Tax records (local): City or County Treasurer, Town Treasurer, City or County Auditor—or other equivalents: in Tennessee, the County Trustee; in New Jersey, the Tax Collector.

Birth and death records: Bureau (or Registrar) of Vital Statistics of the city or county, City or County Clerk, State Health Department.

Marriage records: County Clerk, Clerk of Courts (county), Marriage License Bureau (city).

Local laws: County Clerk, Clerk of Courts.

School records: County or District Superintendent of Schools.

Military records (early militia rolls): County Clerk.

Census records: County Clerk
Judicial records: Clerk of Courts, Office of the Probate
Judge (county or city), or the Surrogate in New York.

Welfare and Social Service department records are not
usually open. Some restrictions are also placed on vital statistics and judicial records, depending on the date and type of
material. In all of these sensitive areas, the individual's right to
privacy is a major consideration, though provision for it is not
uniform.

When asking for records and using them in local depositories, keep in mind that you are not dealing with librarians, but with officials whose main business is with the
more active current records. Your needs will be somewhat exceptional and your patience may be tried before they are met.
You will also often be dealing with political appointees. This
does not necessarily affect their attitude toward you, but it
may mean a higher turnover in staff and a lower degree of
professional skill. Frequently one finds a local official in office
today who is trying to do his best to overcome in a few years
the neglect or incompetence of his predecessors in office for
decades, if not centuries. The usual shortage of proper stor-
age space can make the task impossible without the large
budgets which local governments have typically been lacking
for any purpose in recent years. A shortage of working space
is also typical. But conditions are never impossible, and your
discomfort is widely shared. It helps if you smile a lot.

Any record series normally or first kept in one place may
have been moved to another by the time you are ready for it.
It may be in a municipal or county archives or records center,
or a state archives. Whether or not the state archives contains
records transferred to it from local agencies, it can be expected to hold the records of several state agencies which have
had a strong local impact. Such records are often organized by
county and are therefore quite manageable. It is a safe assumption that the state archives should have something of importance for you whenever you are investigating the history
of a city, town, or county in a fairly comprehensive way. In

some cases you will find that the more recent material you want has not yet arrived at the archives and must be sought in either the state records center (if there is one) or the originating agency. This is an inconvenience but not necessarily a major obstacle, and the state archives is the place where the trail begins and the best guidance is to be found.

Finding the state archives itself is not always simple. It may be an independent state agency listed in the telephone directory under a recognizable name (e.g., public archives commission or department of archives and history), but more often it is less visible. It may be a division of the state library, the state historical society, the secretary of state's office, or the office of general services. An inquiry at the state library or the historical society may be necessary to end the guessing. The one thorough book on the subject, Ernst Posner's *American State Archives,* is no longer a sure guide because of its 1964 publication date. Every state has an official archival agency and service capability. A number are undergoing improvements each year after late starts, and even the weakest may have just what you are looking for.

The Archives Branches of the Federal Records Centers

Federal records of local and regional significance are not, fortunately, all kept in Washington. In fact there is a well-established trend toward keeping them out of Washington. A little publicized but important development of recent years has been the growth of National Archives and Records Service (NARS) regional centers. Known as Federal Archives and Records Centers (FARCs), there are eleven of them outside of Washington which now have archives branches specializing in documents relating to their regions. They are rapidly being stocked not only from the federal agency field office records and the district courts, but through transfers from an overloaded National Archives as well. In addition, each of them is gradually adding microfilm produced under the NARS microfilm publications program. This alone is a potential 74,000,000 pages of records.

Archives Branches of the National Archives
and Records Service

For each of the following, address inquiries to: **Chief, Archives Branch, Federal Archives and Records Center.** If you phone, they are open on weekdays from 8:20, at the latest, to closing time, usually 4:30.

Boston
380 Trapelo Road
Waltham, Mass. 02154
(Telephone 617-223-2657. Serves Connecticut, Maine, Massachusetts, New Hampshire, Rhode Island, and Vermont.)

New York
Building 22—MOT Bayonne
Bayonne, N.J. 07002
(Telephone 201-645-6455. Serves New York, New Jersey, Puerto Rico, Virgin Islands.)

Philadelphia
5000 Wissahickon Avenue
Philadelphia, PA 19144
(Telephone 215-951-9588. Serves Delaware and Pennsylvania; for the loan of microfilm also serves the District of Columbia, Maryland, Virginia, and West Virginia.)

Atlanta
1557 St. Joseph Avenue
East Point, GA 30344
(Telephone 404-763-7476. Serves Alabama, Georgia, Florida, Kentucky, Mississippi, North Carolina, South Carolina, and Tennessee.)

Chicago
7358 South Pulaski Road
Chicago, Ill. 60629
(Telephone 312-353-0164. Serves Illinois, Indiana, Michigan, Minnesota, Ohio, and Wisconsin.)

Denver
Box 25307
Denver, CO 80225
(Telephone 303-234-5271. Serves Colorado, Montana, North Dakota, South Dakota, Utah, and Wyoming.)

San Francisco
1000 Commodore Drive
San Bruno, CA 94066
(Telephone 415-876-9003. Serves northern California, Hawaii, Nevada except Clark County, and the Pacific Ocean area.)

Los Angeles
24000 Avila Road
Laguna Niguel, CA 92677
(Telephone 213-831-4220. Serves Arizona; the southern California counties of Imperial, Inyo, Kern, Los Angeles, Orange, Riverside, San Bernardino, San Diego, San Luis Obispo, Santa Barbara, and Ventura; and Clark County, Nev.)

Seattle
6125 Sand Point Way NE.
Seattle, WA 98115
(Telephone 206-442-4502. Serves Alaska, Idaho, Oregon, and Washington.)

Kansas City
2306 East Bannister Road
Kansas City, MO 64131
(Telephone 816-926-7271. Serves Iowa, Kansas, Missouri, and Nebraska.)

Fort Worth
4900 Hemphill Street (building address)
P.O. Box 6216 (mailing address)

Fort Worth, TX 76115
(Telephone 817-334-5515. Serves Arkansas, Louisiana, New Mexico, Oklahoma, and Texas.)

The specific locations of each Archives Branch and the areas they cover are given in the listing above. What you can expect to find in any given branch varies with the case, but in general these are the types of records common to all branches where there has been activity of the type described.

In addition to these, there are at present three federal records centers holding inactive files (but not archives) for their regions. They are in Washington, D.C.; Dayton, Ohio; and Mechanicsburg, Pennsylvania. Their holdings will be of relatively recent date, and only a fraction of them will ever be transferred to the archives for permanent retention.

Records of the District Courts of the United States. These include criminal, civil, admiralty, and bankruptcy dockets and case files, indexes, and related records. They may date from as early as 1789 to as recently as 1948, depending on the date of a court's establishment. Some branches also have British Vice-Admiralty records, U.S. circuit court records, Confederate district court records, and U.S. territorial court records. U.S. district attorney and marshals' records are also accessioned.

United States Court of Appeals records. At present these include appellate jurisdiction records from 1891 to the mid-1940s.

Bureau of Indian Affairs records. Field office records, censuses, vital statistics, and school records from the mid-nineteenth century to 1952. Additional records, mostly from discontinued agencies and schools dating from before 1900, are in Washington.

Bureau of Customs records. These date between 1790 and 1926 and relate to a variety of port activities including ship movements and the registration of seamen.

Records of the Office of the Chief of Engineers (Army). These include reports, maps, correspondence, and other

records relating to land acquisition, fortification, conserva-
tion, and navigation between 1807 and 1945.

To these should be added the gradually increasing record
files from the field offices of the following agencies: the Interior Department's National Park Service and Bureau of
Land Management, the Agriculture Department's Forest Service and Agricultural Research Service, the Treasury
Department's Internal Revenue Service and Bureau of the
Mint, and the Transportation Department's Coast Guard. In
addition, there are some territorial records in the logically
placed branches such as San Francisco (Samoa, 1899–1945)
and Seattle (Alaska, 1884–1958).

Each of these centers is staffed by capable but busy professionals, and any mail inquiries you have in mind should take
this into account. I would suggest that a reasonable first request would be for information as to whether the center has
records from a given agency for a given period, what description of them they could send, and what access there is to them.
On the basis of the reply, you could then decide whether a
visit would be worthwhile or copies of specific items might be
requested by mail.

There are still many records of local significance in the
National Archives in Washington and there always will be,
since the boundaries between the local and the national are
never neat. But the good news for the local historian now is
that his starting point and best bet should be his regional archives branch. Even when it does not have the original records
requested, it may well have a microfilm copy of the needed
material which can be loaned free to a library close to the user.

Church Records

Even if your research is not directed toward the history of
a particular church, you may have use for church records as
sources of vital statistics, marriage records, or evidence on any
one of a number of issues that stirred the community from
time to time. In early rural settlements and in urban immig-

rant communities, the local church was frequently the leading if not the only regular meeting place which brought whole families together. Although not everyone belonged to a church, status and leadership in the community were more clearly reflected in church leadership than is usually the case today. Organized religion had a greater influence on the outlook and daily lives of our ancestors of 100 and 200 years ago, and the competition for that influence from other organizations was less. In the absence of local newspapers, the church and the law court might be the only forums for a range of local feelings and opinions where some record might be kept of them. Court records naturally sound the discordant notes; church records include evidence of more cooperative activity, although no one has claimed that unruffled harmony is the constant mood of the minutes of church governing boards, whether they be vestrymen, trustees, elders, deacons, or associations of clergymen.

Churches are also useful keepers of statistics on their members. Baptismal records have been especially important right up to the beginning of the twentieth century, when state registration of vital statistics finally became the universal practice. Although never a substitute for census returns, church statistics can add details on population changes and, above all, specific data on changes in individual lives.

If your curiosity leads you to a church that is still active, the obvious key to its records will be the minister, priest, or rabbi in charge. If the church has disbanded or merged, a local clergyman of the same faith should be able to point you to those who can find the records. Clergymen also know the ecclesiastical terms necessary for research of this sort—distinctions among archdioceses, annual meetings, synods, and conferences, for example—and can explain them as your needs appear. Lacking personal access to a helpful clergyman, you can get a copy of the *AASLH Directory of Historical Agencies* and look in the index for an organization dedicated to the denomination's history.

If the denomination itself is extinct, as is the case with the

Shakers (United Society of Believers), the logical place to look first for records is in the region's major historical society libraries. The published *National Union Catalog of Manuscript Collections* lists many such holdings, indexing them by denomination. The Historical Records Survey, conducted nationally in the 1930s by the WPA, covered thousands of individual church records, but only a portion of the inventories were published. The major libraries in your state should have copies of whatever was published, and one of them should have that state's unpublished inventories on deposit.

Another type of record often associated with churches is the cemetery inscription. Sometimes these have been systematically traced or copied by other historians or genealogists. Many abandoned cemeteries remain undocumented, however, and transcribing headstones is a worthwhile project in itself. Because this is an outdoor enterprise not necessarily connected with churches, I have discussed it more fully under the head of Physical Remains.

Business Records

Business history is a specialty in itself, and I can sympathize with the nonspecialist who feels it is none of his affair. The conscientious collection of old company records by many historical agencies over the past generation has not been met with swarms of scholars eager to use them, and perhaps the reason is this understandable hesitance to plunge into a mass of technical and impersonal details with so little hope of emerging any the wiser. Yet there is hope.

Probably the most common situation is that faced by the person trying to gather material for the general history of an area who finds partial records, such as store accounts, which yield a few easily understood details of small transactions but apparently nothing more. There may in fact be nothing more, but until that is a certainty it may be well to suggest some questions that could be put to a book of store accounts: does it give a picture of the stock of goods for sale? Does the stock vary with the seasons? Which goods appear to have been locally produced, and which were imported from some distance? What were the leading items in volume or dollars? Were recognizable names from the community listed among the store's patrons, and if so, what can be learned about their buying habits, their credit, their arrivals and departures from town? Is there more than one type of account kept in the book? Are there advertisements in the local press or notices in early town directories which would help clarify the picture of the business? What can be learned about the proprietor, his work force, and their places in the community? What evidence is there of the impact of periods of boom and bust, war, and similar events in the world beyond the store? Finally, if it is a bookkeeping record that is being studied, it is a good idea to enlist the aid of an accountant or bookkeeper to see what information he might catch, or at least to check others' readings of the accounts.

Reconstructing the history of a single firm or type of local business is a larger order. A considerable variety and volume of records are needed—enough so that the researcher has the incentive to plunge in and learn the business: its technical problems, processes, trade talk, personalities, and organization. *Business biography* is an apt term often applied to such an undertaking, and its accomplishment can be just as satisfying to students of local history as personal biographies. Especially at the local level, personal stories ought to be one of its major ingredients and attractions. Interviews with anyone who ever had even occasional dealings with the firm ought not to be neglected. Consultations with individuals who know the kind of business under study can be useful even if they know nothing of the particular firm. These might include bankers, lawyers, suppliers, and customers as well as veterans of the business itself. In the case of a manufacturer, samples of its products ought to be traced and studied. None of these are substitutes for having the accounts, correspondence, and reports of the firm, but as supplements they are indispensable if the historian is to recreate the life story of the firm in any realistic way.

In any kind of research, one seldom finds just the right amount and kind of material—no more, no less. Company records especially seem to go to extremes: when they are sufficient, they tend to be superabundant as well. The unselected files of even a small firm can sometimes mount over the years to a mountainous bulk. Nevertheless, they are presumably organized in some way related to the structure of the business and the calendar of the years. If you can learn the present structure, you should have a first key to the types of records to look for. Lacking the ideal guide to a particular company, you might use the following checklist as a substitute:

Executive correspondence. Files of the president and other senior officers should provide a view of the company from the front office. Minutes of board meetings and committee meetings should be here if anywhere. Copies of annual reports should be brought to the surface and studied early. Legal documents—charters, franchises, contracts, leases, deeds, and the like—will be here unless there is a separate legal department.

Accounting records. Here should be annual, quarterly, and monthly summaries of many kinds of transactions. These may need to be plucked out from among tons of daily records, but their location will not be random.

Sales records. Here is the story of how the company met its public. Any evidence on the organization, personnel, and methods of selling is always worth attention. Reports on competitors' activities and customers' reactions are also valuable for perspective on the company from the outside.

Advertising material. Records and data describing its creation and use are of obvious interest in conjunction with records of sales performance.

Production records. These may not all be in one place, but the subject ought to be followed carefully whether the production was of goods or services. Pictures, diagrams, and reports by technical staff or consultants on special problems or experiments can all help to fill out the story.

Labor and personnel records. Summaries of activity in this area may be duplicated in the front office records. The more detailed records can be useful for indications of fringe benefits and disciplinary measures in action, and for samplings of individual case histories of earnings, job mobility, turnover, and complaints or disputes.

"Everything is connected with everything else," as the ecologists have been reminding us lately, and the statement is true enough for business historians to make them feel less isolated in taking on a local study than they once did. If you are considering a local tannery or pottery as your subject, be assured that others have written of other tanneries and potteries and of those industries generally. The same is true of virtually any other way to make a dollar you can think of. This is only to say that a great many samples have been studied, not that any industry has been covered and closed to new contributions; far from it. A well-done local business study can have more than local interest, especially if it is done with an awareness of comparable studies elsewhere. *Business History Review,* a scholarly quarterly started more than fifty years ago, is a standard source of leads to work being done in the field, while *Agricultural History* is good within its area. The most comprehensive bibliography for the years covered (through 1959 at present) is the multivolume *Writings on American History,* which is cited in full in the bibliography.

A knotty problem for anyone trying to understand financial transactions from even fifty years ago is that of interpreting prices and wages. Fairly reliable data linking the two at a given time are available starting in the twentieth century, so for this period the question is mainly one of relating the value of a dollar then to a dollar "now"—meaning whenever a reader happens to pick up the book. Since "today's dollar" is hardly a fixed value, and neither wage nor price statistics can be compared accurately or simply over long periods of time, caution is always in order. For the nineteenth century and earlier, the only safe rule is to make no judgments at all on whether anything was expensive or cheap except in relation to something else *at the same time.* For much of our history up to the Civil War, there was not even a standard national currency in practical effect. Regardless of legalisms and face values, a five-dollar bill issued on the credit of an obscure state bank three states away was not accepted in trade at the same worth as a five-dollar gold piece from the U.S. Mint. Such *hard money* or *specie* was always in short supply, and paper money was often suspect even when plentiful because it issued from too many sources. The fate of paper money issued by the Continental Congress and later by the Confederate government is well known. In the colonial period, British currency circulated in company with Spanish, French, and Dutch, and a great many transactions even then were based on barter because none of these or an established credit system were available. In short, a dollar is always worth only what it will buy at the moment and usually all the historian can do is to report what the choices were at any given time and place.

Physical Remains

If the entire stock of the nation's paper, film, and parchment were to dissolve into dust tomorrow, the historian's first duty would be to lend a hand in sweeping the mess up before everyone choked to death. To keep his mind active, meanwhile, he could do worse than to contemplate the variety of source materials that remain for his use. He could begin, belatedly, to think like an archeologist. Anticipating a little, I believe he would come up with at least this conclusion.

American history since the arrival of the white man has taken place within the modern era of Western history, and this means that it has been marked by increasingly rapid changes of two kinds: in technology and in fashion. One or both have modified our heritage of man-made objects since the settlement of Jamestown. Strongly established traditions of folk costumes, building, and crafts are common survivals in older cultures but rare exceptions here. Consequently, the chronology of innovations in technology and fashion is a story so eventful as to be virtually an alternative record to the written one usually consulted. Not only the timing of changes, but also their character may be read in this unwritten record. Ours has been a literate culture from the start, but it has also been an inventive and restless, even a fickle one.

The physical remains of our past encompass every variety of structure, tool, or decoration from a stone fort to a sewing needle. But one must begin somewhere; I will start arbitrarily outdoors. The kind of curiosity the good pedestrian historian develops is equally useful among the relics to be found on shelves and attic floors.

Most local historians need little encouragement to leave the libraries and see for themselves the places where their stories happened. Research often begins on the inspiration sparked by an old house or the ruins of a landmark public building. Only rarely has everything changed enough to discourage those trained to see as historians.

The outdoor historian looking for man marks rather than deer marks might begin in town with a series of walks and a line of questions such as this: (1) what materials have been used here, and why, and from where? (2) What styles mark the structure and adornment of buildings along the way, and what time periods can be assigned to them? (3) What has been planted, either privately or officially, and when? (There is a history of styles in landscaping just as there is in architecture.) (4) What buildings or blocks have been put to different uses since they were built, and why? (5) What changes in transportation have affected the street's inhabitants?

None of these are speculative questions in their nature, although answers may only be approximate or tentative. Satisfactory answers usually require inquiry into both the local records and the more general histories in the library. Sometimes dates are visible on the buildings themselves, either in cornerstones or on façades of public buildings. Remember, though, that a lot of remodeling and expanding can happen without disturbing a cornerstone. And public buildings are not usually

as obscure in origin as private dwellings in any case. That is
one reason it is useful to keep a little architectural history in
your head. With it you can drive down any street in the country and date within twenty-five years or less the development
of each side of each block. You can give names to what you
see, whether you are telling or asking about them.

For example, walking into a typical Ohio county-seat town
along one of its major avenues, the landmarks unfold a
history-in-reverse that might go something like this: first there
is "mortgage row" along the treeless green lawns of the ranch-
styles and split-levels outside the city limits and near the farmers who have subdivided their pastures so the new doctors
and plant managers may have room to graze and breed. Just
inside the city line are a few empty lots before a subdivision of
bland "colonial" brick and frame houses appears, a reminder
of the building spree that followed World War II. Or these
may be scattered over the suburban lots which remained from
the 1920s and '30s. The homes of these years are of several
borrowed styles: the English half-timbered with stucco, shing-
led roofs, and gables; the Spanish or Florida look in stucco or
painted brick; the early ranch, with more porches than later,
and perhaps a porte-cochère; some frame or shingle stock
models with steeply pitched roofs and prominent chimneys;
and perhaps an occasional flat-topped white box arrangement
in the then daring modernistic style.

Closer in, the pre-World War I bungalow appears (note
the front porch), and on the corners there may be relics of the
Queen Anne style and similar late Victorians now kept up as
funeral homes or adapted to office uses. Nearer to downtown
the mid-century gothic survives, perhaps on a building itself
remodeled over an older Greek Revival beginning. In the
same neighborhood there should be an occasional Tuscan villa
with its symmetry and its cupola. Untouched Greek Revival is
scarce, but you may find it within a few blocks of the main
square. In the eastern Midwest it will usually be the oldest
style in evidence, having been the fashion in the years
1830–50. The present county courthouse on the square would

be of a later date; it and a bank or an old hotel might represent a French Renaissance inspiration, with a mansard roof and some sort of tower, from the years of Grant's presidency. If you want to guess when the town was founded, walk through the quiet streets around (not on) the main square; the business center itself will conceal the earlier structures under the waves of subsequent prosperity.

Monuments might be found anywhere in town or out, and in or out of their original locations. A good many are bound to have suffered visibly, but the local historian owes each of them one close look. They all have at least two stories to tell. One is their direct message concerning the event or person they honor. It may be accurate or not, just as with any other source. The other is the local history of the monument itself, which usually needs to be filled out from other sources. Who erected it, when, and where, and what has happened since and why? The *why* is implied in each question, although it may not be answerable. Why did the monument have this sponsor and not others? Why this date and not an earlier or later one? Why was it erected here and not elsewhere? One hopes that there will be some answers, and among them some interesting ones.

Cemetery headstones are monuments of an especially useful sort because they mark burial sites and offer vital statistics as well as honors to the departed. A systematic personal tour of most cemeteries is unnecessary for research purposes. The grounds that are being maintained will have records which may be consulted on request; a telephone call or two should be sufficient to make an appointment. Even abandoned cemeteries may have had their inscriptions recorded and placed on deposit at the historical society or library. If there is no written guide available and you want to consider preparing one, consult the leaflet by John J. Newman cited in the bibliography. His advice is worth noting even if you are making a search only for selected markers. Newman illustrates some of the common reading problems and prepares the investigator to meet a whole range of obstacles.

An eye for historical change can be developed in the coun-
tryside as well as in town. Not along the modern expressways,
where nothing but direction signs are allowed to remain in the
foreground, but along the older highways and roads, traveling
can be an eventful experience for the historian looking for
signs of the past in the present. The land itself may be read by
those who understand something of water tables, soils and
drainage, the stages of forest succession, and some varieties of
farm practice and malpractice. Virgin forest is an extremely
rare sight from any road in the United States, and if any of
the tall grass prairie of the upper Midwest remains, it is in a
small patch in Missouri that may have been divided by a new
highway by now. Streambeds change, of course, and you may
see more man-made ponds and reservoirs than nature ever
provided without the assistance of bulldozers.

One could add examples for pages, but the point to be
made here is that these are not merely events in natural history beyond the scope of the nonscientist. They are events in
the history of human land use, and they are as important to
the historian as a stage is to the playwright. Especially if your
home territory is partly rural, you will want to study the
changes in the landscape over the years. There are books that
can help, there are old residents, and perhaps the county extension agent has ideas. With their aid, the subject can gradually become less baffling and more fascinating, especially if
you persist in making your own firsthand observations. Sometimes good research requires good legs and hiking boots.

Returning from a long hike and shedding his boots, the
physical remains of the local historian might be ready to relax
in the contemplation of his own living room. Whether his
home is old or not, its interior has probably changed far more
often and drastically than its exterior. What did such a living
room look like fifty or a hundred years ago? Historic preser-
vationists have had better luck in saving the outsides of old
homes, where nobody ever lived, than the insides, which are
so often scattered among musuem exhibits of coverlets,
thundermugs, desks, cradles, spinning wheels, and sofas. To

reassemble accurately the home environment of an earlier day is difficult, expensive, and rarely well done. It is not realistic to expect every major period to be reconstructed in every county, much less every town.

Fortunately, there are types worth studying on visits afield, and there is the human faculty of imagination. Restorations of early twentieth-century homes are relatively rare, and the ones I am most familiar with are strongly dominated by the personalities of their famous owners—the pretentiousness of Frederick Vanderbilt, the energy and old-family pride of Franklin Roosevelt, and the sometimes predatory energies of Theodore Roosevelt, whose Oyster Bay home contains by my count eighteen big-game trophy heads. Yet each home also reflects some of the shared taste of its time. Lincoln's Springfield home is convincingly restored to the middle-class decorum of his pre-Presidential years, and his New Salem Village evokes the marginal existence of the Illinois pioneers, especially if visited in the cooler months. I have not seen a sod house of the short-grass prairies (they still exist), and until I do I must rely on pictures and on the writings of Ole Rölvaag and others who were there when sod houses were a standard design. When I get to Plymouth, Massachusetts, I will be in the debt of John Demos for his study of Pilgrim family life (*A Little Commonwealth*) which relates the people to their dwellings in an especially persuasive way. Both of these writers (Rölvaag in his novel, *Giants in the Earth*) offer something few restored buildings invite their visitors to experience directly, and that is a feel for the place in winter, without electricity, central heating, plumbing, or running water.

At several village restorations there have been experiments in bringing families to live several days as the original settlers did, and the idea seems worth pursuing. A week's vacation roughing it in the style of 1700, 1800, or 1900 could be exotic, educational, and a good deal less expensive than most vacations promising comparable novelty.

Lacking the advantages of such an experience, the historian must compensate with some imagination if he is to appreciate the daily uses and routines that bring the isolated artifacts of the museums to life. I am sure I would find a candle mold an intensely interesting device if its product stood between me and darkness. An oil lamp would appear in a new light, a kerosene lamp would be seen as the major advance it was, and the electric bulb would come as a shock and a wonder.

Insight into the work routines and basic survival requirements of any past era are only part of the story. They should lead in turn to a new rapport with its play, its sports, and its esthetic tastes. None of our ancestors worked all the time, and in the broad sense none of them stayed sober all the time. The connections that exist in any society between work and play, routine and romance, are elusive at best. They can never be grasped by scholars who look at only one side of life and ignore others on the excuse that they are specialists. We all specialize—necessarily so, in such a large field—but it may be valid to consider specialization as much a confession of a deficiency as a claim to expertise. A barber is also a specialist, but I have never known one to devote his attention exclusively to the back of a customer's head while ignoring the top and sides.

Becoming overspecialized means becoming pedantic and pointless. It is not a danger inherent in the field of local history. Properly understood, as Clifford Lord so often and aptly put it, the field is *localized* history. It is as big as the people doing it. If by definition it lacks breadth, it can make up for that in height and depth. In these dimensions there need be no limits.

CHAPTER TWO

Writing

THINK back over the writing you have already done. Consider not only your more formal efforts like school exercises and magazine articles, but your love letters, condolence letters, vacation letters, and indignant letters to editors.

When you were most effective in communicating—and when you found the greatest satisfaction in the process—there were probably two main reasons for it. You knew your subject well enough to feel some confidence in what you had to write, and you cared enough to want to write with directness and emphasis. In short, you were unusually ready and willing. Since the purpose of this chapter is to encourage you to surpass your previous best efforts, and to extend them over a more ambitious project than you may have attempted before, these questions of readiness and willingness deserve a closer look.

Any writing project begins as a private affair and ends, hopefully, as a public one. Only you can decide when to start putting words on that first sheet of white paper, and only you need look at them. You can face the world later; first you need confidence enough to face your own thoughts and find the words to put them in. But by the time you have achieved that confidence you should have answered satisfactorily in your own mind a few questions about your condition of readiness. If you know your subject well enough to know what it may contain that would interest others, you will be ready for such questions. Here are some of them.

What form is your information in? Is it available on note cards or sheets that can be shuffled around easily as you organize your story? Is some of it in file folders, and if so are they thin enough to allow you to find what you need quickly? How much of it is stored in your head, or in the heads of people you will still need to interview? (Heads are not reliable places to store factual data in large quantities. Magnetic tape is good for short periods; paper is best of all.) The purpose of this whole line of questioning is to urge you to get your raw material into the kind of physical shape that will allow it to serve your needs. If you are not satisfied with the situation, you might look back to the section called Taking Notes and Copying Documents.

Do you have a good idea of how large a subject you have, and how it might best be subdivided? That is, can you sketch an outline of the topics you feel ready to treat, and show how they can be related in a sequence? Can you estimate how many words (and pictures and maps) might be justified, topic by topic? The length of the final product you want depends partly on the scope of your story and the materials you want to include, but equally important is your answer to the next question.

Can you decide what readers you want to reach? Don't laugh: I mean what type of reader you *most* want to reach. There is really no such creature as the "general reader." Book reviewers may use the term out of laziness. Publishers use the term in advertising because they don't want any prospective customers to feel left out. But publishers who have not analyzed their markets to clarify more distinct types of customers soon go into bankruptcy and out of publishing. Here are some informal sketches of the specific publics you might consider as your primary buyers or readers.

1. Dedicated and knowledgeable students of your subject who will read anything you would read yourself. There are never more than a handful of these for local historians. Your carbon copies alone would glut the market.

2. Adults with a real interest in at least some aspect of your subject and a willingness to read about it at some length if the story is attractively presented and sensibly organized. These are not uncritical fans, but they will meet you half way. Readers of historical journals, frequenters of public libraries, and many old residents would be part of this group; by occupation they would include a high proportion of teachers and independent professional people. This is the hard core that you need to reach to justify any effort at publication for adults. Even then you cannot expect it to be a sizeable group at any one time. Numbers add up over a ten- or twenty-year period, however, and publications directed to such a group should be kept available longer than most. This group may be expected to buy especially heavily at the time of a centennial celebration or comparable event.

3. Adults, usually affluent, sharing some interests with members of the last group except that they read virtually nothing of a serious nature longer than a newspaper story. This group is susceptible to books with good pictures in quantity, stylish covers, and well-planned promotions. In many cases a perfectly serious and solid book may be designed with this group in mind as a secondary market. No compromise with the essential integrity of the work need be made, though production costs may run higher.

4. A juvenile readership. This is really a large and ill-defined category which should be clarified with the help of local teachers or librarians who work with children and their books regularly and successfully. There are vast differences between the reading levels and interests of third graders and seventh graders. Our own memories of what we liked at those ages are not entirely to be trusted.

5. Adults living or working outside the locality or special topic you are describing. This would be a sophisticated group that only a sophisticated writer could expect to reach with a subject of wide potential appeal. These people are not interested in local history, but will read about some-

thing that occurred in your community if it appeals to another interest already established in them—e.g., the Raw West and the Real Indian, Lincoln, the Great Battle of—— (which was the turning point of the —— War), the Bloody Strike, Massacre, and Riot of ——, and so on. This is a large readership for local history. Prospective library sales outside your immediate vicinity would be one measure of its size, and potential appeal to hobbyists or cultists is another. A university press or a commercial publisher should be considered likely to be attracted to a work directed to any combination of likely purchasers above five thousand.

Except for the obvious extremes represented by groups one and five, the size of these distinctive publics for history must be estimated locally by those who know the territory. Discuss the matter with individuals whose opinions you respect. Try to make clear to them what you feel you might realistically attempt, and get several reactions. Keep your guard up for those who would simply tell you what they think you want to hear. You can safely enjoy flattery after the work is finished, but until that time it is to be avoided as the original dangerous drug.

The point I want to make with the hypothetical examples above is that early decisions on intended readership, length, style, and content are important even if they are later revised, as many are. Such decisions start the author in a rational way, with at least a sketch map of the entire ground between today's idea and tomorrow's—or next year's—publication.

Some of the possible decisions at this early, tentative stage are suggested in the following numbered paragraphs. These are hypothetical examples phrased in general terms solely as indications of how one can "see" a publication well before it is begun.

1. A series of biographical articles of about 1,000 words each on nationally prominent figures with important local connections, written for the newspaper along lines agreed

upon with the editor. One to three pictures are needed for each sketch, and they must be suitable for newspaper reproduction. Two articles will require maps, which means recruiting talent to execute them.

2. A brief historical sketch of the growth of the community since its founding, hitting the high points of widest interest, and limited to 6,000 words with ten or twelve pictures. This could be a paperback booklet, printed attractively but economically, to be given away to newcomers. Explore the possibility of purchase at cost of a quantity for giveaways by an organization with a budget for such an undertaking. Consider inviting advertisements or help from the local historical society. (Don't expect firm commitments, but if the prospects seem reasonably encouraging, proceed with the writing and show the results in manuscript.)

3. A picture album organized around a fine collection of photographs taken of local scenes from 1900 to 1915 (or some other period). A selection of about thirty pictures would fit into a 36-page, 6-by 9-inch booklet with room for some introductory test. Research on the pictures would be needed to provide captions tying them to the facts. The introductory text would explain briefly the source of the pictures and should be accompanied by an evocative word picture of the community and its patterns of life at the time. Expected readership would be groups two and three above.

4. An article on the rise and fall of the shipbuilding industry in one town. Try for the quarterly journal of the state historical society (group two above, plus scholars interested in maritime history). This means a limit of about 6,000 words, careful documentation, and the use of a few pictures if available.

5. A comprehensive history of the city and its suburbs. The writing would be done by a team of contributors with the senior author given final editorial review of each contribution. Assignments and deadlines would be given according to a plan calling for 90,000 words of text, a section of appendices (documents, lists of officials) requiring twenty pages, four

groups of pictures running eight pages each, three specially drawn maps, and a thorough index. Financing and marketing would be handled by a separate committee representing the local historical society. Expected readership would include groups one, two, and three and libraries with local history collections, including a probable twenty outside the state.

It is tempting to add more examples, but the point is not to suggest what might actually be done so much as to suggest how the starting writer should see his project at this stage. Examples of most types of worthwhile writing projects are in the libraries and should be consulted. If they are studied as lessons rather than ideals to be imitated, they can stimulate the imagination rather than confine it.

Readiness, then, means planning and research, both carried far enough along to enable you to see the outline of the contents and the shape of the final publication.

After readiness comes willingness. Unfortunately, it does not always come easily to those who should start writing. What motivates the person to move from research and planning to actual composition? In the case of local history the motive is not often money, since anyone can make more of it doing almost anything else. More likely it is the same feeling for the subject that motivated the research. Something about the subject fuels the curiosity with emotion. It matters little what the emotion is—affection, amusement, awe, indignation, or even disgust. The stimulus is what counts. Nothing good has ever been written out of boredom.

A second motive might be weak in the novice writer but it must gain strength soon if the writing is to be strong. This is an involvement in the craftsmanship of writing, or, in different words, an enthusiasm for effective communication in writing. Of course, writing is an art and success is ultimately measured against the objectives of art. But the art is founded on the craft, and it is only the craft that can be discussed to any advantage in a book of shop talk such as this one.

You will know you are taking the craft seriously when you become willing to accept criticism, rewrite, and even reorganize. If you have the patience to follow through on these steps, then you have the makings of a writer. If you lack the patience or interest, your work will suffer this time and in the future.

To those who are ready and seriously willing to write history, the impetus should come without much question. Ability will not come suddenly, of course, but in gradual stages as you gain experience and give your attention to it. One of the most useful experiences, incidentally, is to see your work in print. Then as never before you will feel you have been tested and exhibited in public view. What you originally did well, what you got right with an editor's help, and what you left unclear or weak—all these will impress themselves on your mind more forcibly than ever when you see them in their final published form.

Along with your own experience—the school of hard knocks—you can have available the experience of others. It is no substitute, but you would hardly be reading this far in this book if you failed to see its value as a supplement. The experience of others comes in three shapes, which for convenience might be labeled models, exhortations, and conventions. The remainder of this section will take up each of them, the first separately and the latter two more or less together.

Models are simply examples of good writing wherever you find them. Go back to an article or book of history you have previously read and admired. Try to pinpoint the qualities you found especially strong and then see if you can determine how they got there. Every effect has a cause somewhere, but if a particular one escapes you, come back to the problem next year and meanwhile pursue what can be caught with less effort. Some effort is needed in every case, however, since what I am urging on you is rhetorical analysis, which is a form of thinking. Two cautions may be in order. One is that it is natural and quite common for a writer to jump to superficial conclusions on first attempting an analysis of this kind. Check your first inspiration against your second. Give yourself some argument. It may save disappointment later when you come to the real test, which is the application of the lesson to your own writing. Another caution—confine this kind of exercise, at least at first, to models of historical writing reasonably close in time and scope to what you are attempting yourself. Edward Gibbon's *Decline and Fall of the Roman Empire* (6 volumes, 1776–88), for example, is best admired from a distance.

Then there are the conventions to be learned—the etiquette of published writing. Like the etiquette guides of Emily Post, the accepted usages of historical writing change slowly with time and vary slightly with occasion. Some appear to be arbitrary; nearly always they are stated in the form of such brusque, peremptory commands that you may well doubt their reasonableness. But for the most part the conventions are reasonable; the logic behind them is real, and if the logic is rarely discussed in print it is more often to avoid tedium than to forestall argument. In any case, whether a given practice is ideally suited to the historian's purpose or not, consistency in form is itself a virtue because it frees the reader from distractions. Acceptance of the conventions in details has the further practical advantage of making your work more acceptable to editors. If your manuscript is too eccentric in matters of punctuation, capitalization, footnote and bibliography style, a busy editor is likely to simply reject it and leave you with no readers at all.

The reference shelf of any writer should include one or several of the better handbooks of style. The bibliography includes several recommended works, all of them more thorough in coverage of details and special cases than the discussion below, which is a supplement only. Only the three areas of most common concern for historical writing—quotation, documentation, and bibliography—will be treated in the following pages. Because they are important, explanations of the conventions involved will be salted with some exhortations on how they can be most effectively used.

Quotations

Most novices at historical writing quote too often and at too great length, putting too much burden on the words of others. Remember that for the reader a quotation is a kind of interruption. Keep it brief and urgent unless you are presenting it as a document you wish to analyze for the reader. And remember that no matter how impressive the expert you quote in support of a view, no quotation of authority can finally prove any point in a logical argument. It may be persuasive, but it cannot be conclusive.

Probably no quotation of more than a short phrase is ever really *necessary* to any writer's story—again excepting the document inserted as a subject for analysis. Yet a well chosen quotation can add liveliness, flavor, or conciseness where nothing else will do as well. Choosing a good quotation means, of course, confining it to the subject immediately at hand. Never add expendable wordage, no matter how interesting.

Two suggestions may help in reducing a quotation's tendency to interrupt the flow of ideas. The source about to be quoted should first be introduced to the reader, even if in a very general way, and quickly. It prepares the reader for what follows, and incidentally keeps the tone of the passage more conversationally informal. Some examples follow.

The state responded so enthusiastically to the cause that, as the Governor wrote to a friend, it seemed "easier to raise a regiment out here than an acre of corn."[4]

Where had the money gone? Jones pleaded innocence and ignorance: "Damned if I know!" he shouted to the committee the next day.[5]

The third witness reported something still different. From the window over the porch he "saw just the two men, one of them tall and kind of stooped and unsteady as he walked."[6]

Exact citations of sources (as noted 4, 5, and 6 at end of each cited example) would be left to the footnotes, which interrupt only those readers especially interested in them at the moment.

Ellipses. To indicate that you have omitted a word or words, whether within a quotation or at one end of it, use three spaced dots on the line. If you use them at the end of a sentence, they follow the period. Thus: "That's what the man said. . . . But who listens?" is condensed from this longer quotation: "That's what the man said. He told them in plain words and loudly enough, too. But who listens?" A comma or similar end mark is usually treated the same way as the period—it goes first. The rule is firm about the number of dots, or ellipsis points, as they are called. More than three, except as other punctuation requires, is bad manners. On the rare occasions when you omit words from a quotation and pick up again in a later paragraph, you should mark the ellipsis where you break off, skip a line, indent for the new paragraph, and then proceed. If your new start is at any point beyond the opening word of the new paragraph, you need a new set of dots to indicate that omission. The previous set was only good for the previous paragraph. This is complicated, but if you insist on long quotations you have to bear the consequences.

Do not feel that ellipsis points are necessary where the reader should have sense enough to recognize the fragment without help. Proverbial phrases, clichés, a line from the Lord's Prayer, and a repetition of part of something you have just quoted at length, are examples of self-evident fragments. The three quotations on the previous page are also examples.

End Punctuation. Here is the rule on punctuating the end of a quotation: tuck your comma or period *inside* the final quotation mark, for appearance's sake. (The English do it differently, and their independence is to be respected, but here you are given the American Way.) All other punctuation (!?:;) falls outside the closing quotation mark unless it is part of the material being quoted. Thus "Where was he?" quotes a question, including its mark. But to ask you, aren't we trying to "unscrew the inscrutable"? is to make my own question out of a borrowed phrase.

Quotations within Quotations. It would be confusing to keep the same double quotation marks around words being quoted within a quoted passage, so they are changed to single marks: "He said, 'They're all crazy'; those were his words."

Brackets. The main use of brackets is to enclose your own words within a quoted passage; they are not part of the quotation. They are seldom needed, but when they are, there is no substitute. Draw them in by hand if necessary, but avoid the temptation to accept parentheses in substitution just because they appear on your typewriter keys. Parentheses are interpreted as having been in the quoted material originally. Thus, "He said (in an undertone) that he [General Grant] had just arrived." Here the author being quoted is responsible for the parenthetical phrase. The writer doing the quoting has inserted the General's name in brackets to identify clearly the second "he." Brackets are properly used for enclosing any editorial insertions of your own in passages you quote—comments, corrections, missing words, translations, and so on. If you should quote a passage which itself contains bracketed words, there appears to be no way you can prevent the reader from becoming confused short of offering an explanatory note following your footnoted source citation.

Brackets have another common use, most often in footnote and bibliographical citations rather than in quoted matter: they serve to mark parentheses within parentheses.

Long Quotations. Occasionally, despite all cautions, you will feel you must quote an extended passage. If it runs to ten or so lines, the reader may forget he is reading quoted matter before he finishes.[1] To prevent such confusion, the entire passage should be set off in a format distinct from the remainder of the page. The customary way is to omit the quotation marks and single space between lines with paragraph indention at the left margin of every line (or both left and right, if the

---

1. Ten lines are suggested here as the breaking point, but there is no agreement among the style books on any exact number. Some authorities urge five lines, others as many as fourteen. The reasoning is the same in every case, but its application is a matter for the author and his editor to determine. They should be the best judges of what it takes to confuse their readers.

resulting line is not excessively short). In typing copy for the printer, make the indention but continue double spacing; then simply mark in the margin the closer spacing you want him to follow in typesetting.

Quoting Verse and Song. These have predetermined line lengths, and so are a special case. Even two lines may be set off, centered left and right, and four or more should be so treated for greatest readability. In short quotations, the end of a line of verse may be marked by a slash (solidus, to be formal) to save space or to diminish the prominence of the quotation. Thus: "Breathes there the man with soul so dead/ who never to himself hath said,/ 'This is my own, my native land! . . .' " The end punctuation here is a bit more complicated than usual, but it has to show that I have not quoted the entire poem (thus ellipsis points) but have ended the speaker's sentence, the poet's line, and my quotation.

When omitting one or more whole lines from a verse or poem, use one full line of spaced ellipsis points to show the gap. This is an exception to the limit of three points.

Documentation

Either in your notes or in the books around you, exact citations should be available to support every quotation or statement of fact that goes into your writing. How and when to use them in writing for publication is another question. The answer as to *when* depends on two considerations. One is the obligation of a courtesy credit to those originating the quotations, ideas, and graphic materials you are using. The other is the curiosity of your reader. Both of these considerations deserve some elaboration.

Courtesy—Optional and Required. You should want to acknowledge your borrowings in any case where an omission might possibly give some readers the impression that you are claiming something as your own unfairly. Since your borrowed material is sometimes valuable property, the law requires recognition of its creators' interests in several ways. You should acquire at least a layman's understanding of the laws of plagiarism, copyright, and libel. It is quite possible to run afoul of any of them without the slightest criminal intention.

This is especially true of *plagiarism,* which is the adoption of another writer's words presented as if they were your own. Even with some changes in wording, the result legally may be a plagiarism. Neither your exact reproduction of the original language nor the original author's copyright on the material lifted is necessary to make a charge of plagiarism stick. To avoid this kind of trouble, first take care in your note taking that you indicate quotation marks carefully, so that later you are sure of what was copied verbatim. Second, be sure that when you paraphrase, you really paraphrase. For further reading on plagiarism, including some interesting case histories, see the book by Alexander Lindey in the bibliography.

Copyright: Published Works. When a publication is copyrighted, its owner in effect stakes his claim and gives warning to those who might take unearned profits from his labors or reduce his chances of earning profits. If your intended quotation might have such an effect—as it well could, if you quoted a page of prose or any complete unit, such as a poem or a song, a chart or a graph—you should write to the copyright owner or the publisher of the work quoted, requesting permission to quote. Indicate the exact passage used, with page numbers and title of the work where it is found; list purpose and title of your own work, its approximate length, publisher, and expected date of publication. Permission to quote is not required for (1) publications of the federal government or those of most states—documents normally dedicated to public use from the outset—but check these for a possible copyright notice; (2) publications dated 1976 or earlier, carrying no copyright notice; or (3) publications on which the copyright has expired.

Determining whether a copyright has expired can sometimes be complicated. Since January 1, 1978, when the new U.S. Copyright Act of 1976 went into effect, earlier copyright guidelines have become obsolete.

Copyright protection now lasts longer than it used to. Supplanting the old law's twenty-eight years from date of publication plus twenty-eight years more if copyright was renewed, the new law protects works created on or after January 1, 1978, for the duration of the author's life plus fifty years; for older works properly renewed, it extends the renewal term to forty-seven years, lengthening total copyright protection for older works to seventy-five years. What may seem arbitrary time periods in discussion of the new law actually reflect complex mergings of old and new terms of coverage, put into operation by several special acts of Congress until enactment of the new law, which was long in gestation.

Here are some new guidelines:

1. If the copyright date in question is 1905 or earlier, that copyright has expired; the work is in the public domain.

2. Works copyrighted *before* September 19, 1906, have also expired; however, those copyrighted *from September 19, 1906, on,* through December 31, 1949, if properly renewed under the old law—and until a search by the Copyright office indicates otherwise, you have to assume that they *were* renewed—are now protected until the end of the seventy-fifth year from the date of original copyright: December 31, 1981, for valid 1906 copyrights; December 31, 2024, for those secured in 1949, and so on.

3. Works copyrighted between January 1, 1950, and December 31, 1977, would have been in their first term when the new law took effect. Their renewal terms, if applied for at the proper time, run for forty-seven years instead of the old twenty-eight-year renewal. That would extend coverage of a 1950 copyright through 2025; but these renewals must be applied for as the first term nears its end; otherwise, coverage expires after the original twenty-eight years, and the work is in the public domain.

4. Works copyrighted in 1978 and since are protected for the author's lifetime plus fifty years. Coverage begins from the date a work is completed, even if it has not yet been published. Further, coverage is automatic for the first five years, even if the work carries no copyright notice. Beyond five years, formal copyright registration is required. These new, more lenient provisions regarding notice placement and registration dates replace the

earlier common-law copyright protections eliminated by the 1976 law.

You can learn whether registration has occurred only by inquiring at the Copyright Office. To avoid guesswork about any copyright question, telephone or use the mails. The Copyright Office, Library of Congress, Washington, D.C. 20559, will send their pamphlet, *How to Investigate the Copyright Status of a Work*, free, on request. In writing to publishers, direct inquiries to the firm's rights and permissions department. Addresses of publishers appear in the current issue of *Literary Market Place*, available in most libraries.

Copyright: Unpublished Works. For unpublished works, old copyright regulations included a common-law right of protection, *in perpetuity*. Thus, a letter, diary, photograph, poem, or thesis might be given away, sold, or passed through many hands without any rights to reproduction or publication of any part of the work accompanying such transfers: rights in the content belonged only to the originator or his heirs. No one else owned anything but the paper the work appeared on and control of access to it, unless other rights dealing with content were transferred separately. No copyright registration or warning notice was necessary. The new law does not provide such perpetual coverage, but there is coverage enough for our working lifetime: rights of authors (or photographers or artists) of even very old unpublished works will not expire before the year 2002, and works created—that is, completed, on paper—from 1978 on are given the same lifetime-plus-fifty-years protection as published works.

Libel. You are allowed to criticize and even misrepresent someone in the words or pictures you produce, but if you do so in a way that damages him in the legal sense, you may be subject to a suit for libel. Only the living can bring suit for damages to themselves, and they can win their case only if the damage was caused by misrepresentation of the facts. Truth is a defense. No historian who takes care in handling his facts need be afraid of libel suits arising from the impact of his facts on someone's reputation. You cannot control or predict suits that may be brought against you on inadequate grounds, but you can guard your writing to make sure you will win if you should be brought to court. Paul B. Ashley's book on libel is listed in the bibliography for those who feel they may have a problem.

Your readers will be justifiably curious to know where you found the material that is new and worthwhile in your story. It is one of your obligations as a writer to foresee and meet such expectations. If your research notes are in good order, the burden is not usually very great. A large number of facts, sayings, quoted phrases, definitions, and summaries of ideas may be passed on to the reader on your own authority as the author simply because they are common enough knowledge and easily checked should they be in error. Beyond this point documentation may be called for even if it is given informally in the text, as it might be in a newspaper article.

The reader who is casual or hurried is generally willing to trust the author's authority and judgment. He just wants the story. Even if he quarrels with some detail of it he has no intention of following up footnote references. But the scholar, the hobbyist, and anyone reading a reference work is likely to be far more curious as to the source of anything he finds controversial. The scholar likes to see citations of sources even when he has no intention of following them up himself. It is one way he evaluates the authority of what he is reading, and properly so.

Not every reader's whim can be satisfied, but the legitimate inquiry can be anticipated. To repeat for emphasis: document clearly whatever you are writing that may be relatively new or controversial in the eyes of your readers, but do not trouble yourself to reassure them of the obvious and the commonplace.

Footnotes

The footnote is still the most common form of source citation.[2] It is a highly refined and useful invention, even

2. There is also the purely explanatory footnote, which is useful for an author's

though it has often been crudely and pointlessly used. Once you become accustomed to its uses and construction (if you are not already), you will appreciate its value in conveying the right amount of information at the right place in a highly concise way.

After you have decided to use footnotes, the next question is how to mark them in the text. The safest and most common sign is a number in a series running consecutively through the chapter or article. (An asterisk will serve the purpose only if you are sure you will be using only very occasional notes—one every few pages.) The number is printed above the line where it cannot be confused with other numbers. Insert it where it will interrupt the reader least, but keep it close to the material it refers to. One obvious place is at the end of a quotation. If, however, you paraphrase the source quoted for a clause or sentence following the actual quotation, hold the footnote signal until the end of the paraphrase. In short, try to wait until you have finished using that source. When a paragraph or more is based on a single source, the reference may be held for citation at the end with a brief explanation of what it covers. For example, such a footnote might read:

> The above account of Watson's youth is based on C. Vann Woodward, *Tom Watson, Agrarian Rebel* (New York: Oxford University Press, Galaxy ed., 1963), pp. 12–31.

The same technique may be used where two sources are referred to, provided you add further clarification of the specific connection between the text and the sources. In general, you can reduce the number of footnotes by letting each of them carry all the information it can hold without losing clarity.

Keeping track. Footnoting is most conveniently done as part of the development of the first draft, while you are still close

---

digressions, definitions, and cross references. Such explanatory matter may also be added to a source footnote remarking on the nature of the source or other matters at hand. What you are reading now is an explanatory footnote.

to your source notes. Because at this point you do not know where the foot of your finished or printed page will be, there is no advantage in putting notes at the foot of the page of draft. The simplest way to handle them in draft is to insert them in parentheses at the point in the text where they will be referred to, setting them off with a signal to yourself such as the word NOTE. Numbering can wait until revisions are complete and retyping is in order. (NOTE: This is the form I mean. Numbering is unnecessary at this stage because there is no separation of text and footnote.) If you want to add visibility to your note, circle the entire thing with a red pencil after it is out of the typewriter. The advantage in this method is that by keeping the note in sight you minimize the risk of forgetting to modify it should you revise the text.

Numbers can be assigned to footnotes just before the final typing. If the final copy is being prepared for setting in type by a printer, be sure to move all footnotes to a separate series of sheets for each chapter, giving them the proper heading and attaching them at the end of the chapter of text. The printer will set them in a different size of type and place them in position on the proper pages when he makes up the page forms.

Backnotes. These are notes kept together in a separate section at the back of the book, just ahead of the index. The added expense of having the printer fit footnotes in place on each page is largely responsible for the growing popularity of backnotes as an alternative at least for source citations.

Constructing Footnotes

Good source notes have at least three virtues: They are clear, concise, and consistent. These are the aims of the conventions and suggestions given below. For special problems not covered here, consult the latest edition of the University of Chicago Press's *Manual of Style*, which is the most thorough work of its kind.

First References. You first citation of a source must be the most complete; in fact, it may take the place of a bibliographical listing when the work is an article or short book. Second and subsequent references to a source are given more briefly in the forms shown in the following section. First references take different forms according to type of material—book, periodical, government document, manuscript or archival collection.

Books

First references should include the following in the order given:

1. Author's name. If no author is given, the institutional sponsor, or editor or compiler goes here, but the latter two should be labeled as such so as not to be presented as authors. If an author has used a pen name, enclose his real name, if you know it, in brackets immediately after it. See examples below. Never reverse the order of a name in a footnote, since you are not alphabetizing.

2. Complete title of the book. The only place where you are sure to find this is on the title page. If there is a subtitle, separate it from the main title by a colon unless other punctuation is given. You will be forgiven for using ellipsis points (three) to shorten excessively long titles. (Until this century it was not unusual for title pages to be crowded with material that went beyond announcement and into advertisement.) *Underline* the title, whether it is to appear in print (where it will be in italics) or remain in typescript.

3. Editor, compiler, or translator, if any. His name may be preceded or followed by his function. If his name comes first, his function may be abbreviated and put in parentheses: (ed.), (comp.), or (trans.). The other order would be: ed. by ———, and so on.

4. Title of series in which the book appears, if any, followed by the volume or number designation in the series.

5. Edition used, if later than the first, or if paperback rather than hard-cover edition. The specification of the

paperback edition not only calls attention to its availability but covers you in case the pagination is different.

6. Number of volumes, if more than one.

7. City where published, including the state, abbreviated, if the city is small or not unique: Portland, Ore., Springfield, Ill., etc. If no place of publication is given, use the abbreviation "n.p." here.

8. Publisher, if permission to quote is involved; otherwise this is optional. You should have the publisher's name in your notes for use in the bibliography in any case, and its use in a footnote sometimes adds a useful clue to the character of a book.

9. Year of publication. This is the year of the edition used, and is normally found on the title page and on the page following, with the copyright date. If you find only copyright dates, use the most recent. If you know the year of publication but it does not appear in the book, enter it in brackets. If you only think you know, use brackets and a question mark. If you know you don't know, enter the abbreviation "n.d." for "no date."

10. Volume and page(s) cited. This is the last item in the footnote reference, and because its location identifies it, there has been a trend toward simplifying it by eliminating the abbreviations vol. and p. or pp., and the use of roman numerals for the volume number. Thus volume III, page 27, may be cited simply as 3:27, the colon separating them. The 27 alone would indicate that page in a one-volume work. If you cite two or more pages as a group, write 27–29. This means you are including 28; if you want to cite 27 and 29, but not 28, use a comma: 27, 29. Large numbers are not repeated in their entirety if there is no chance of confusion, but you should give the last two digits unless the first of them is a zero: 269–71 or 1006–11.

Examples of first citations of books. Note that these are given in their fullest form on the assumption that no bibliography is to be added at the end. If you are adding a bibliography, the inclusion of the publisher is optional except where permission from one is involved. (Second citations of publications are in briefer forms. See pages 89-90.).

1. Norman F. Cantor and Richard I. Schneider, *How to Study History* (New York: Thomas Y. Crowell, c. 1967), 15.
   —Uncomplicated except for joint authorship. Note comma placement before the title, date and page number, but not before the material in parentheses. The "c. 1967" means that no date appears on the title page, so the copyright date (normally found on the reverse of the title page) has been cited instead.

2. University of Chicago Press, *A Manual of Style*, 12 ed., rev. (Chicago and London: University of Chicago Press, 1969), 357.
   —Institutional sponsor takes the place of the unidentified authors of this collaborative work. Listing the second headquarters city of the publisher is optional.

3. Benjamin P. Thomas, *Portrait for Posterity: Lincoln and His Biographers* (New Brunswick, N.J.: Rutgers University Press, 1947), 22–23, 39.
   —Colon provided to set off subtitle; state added for New Brunswick; 3 pages cited.

4. Thomas R. Frazier (ed.), *Afro-American History: Primary Sources,* shorter ed. (New York: Harcourt Brace Jovanovich, 1971), 259.
   —Editor and edition are both abbreviated "ed." This firm's four other headquarters cities have been omitted.

5. Beverley W. Bond, Jr., *The Foundations of Ohio* (Volume I [1941] of Carl Wittke, ed., *The History of the State of Ohio,* 6 vols., Columbus: Ohio State Archaeological and Historical Society, 1941–46), 260.
   —Because this volume would be cataloged under its separate title by librarians, it could be located by a searcher who did not know that it is volume I of a set. You could omit the set here if you included it in a bibliographical listing at the end. But including it here also could be an aid in finding the book, and it establishes a helpful association with a standard title. Note also that the place of publication omits *Ohio* because the name of the publisher locates it clearly.

6. Clifford W. Browder [Axel R. Angstrom], *Reminiscences of Old Greenfield* (Greenfield, N.D.: the author [1946]), 39.

—Pen name: *privately printed* would also indicate that the author was the publisher. The year of publication was determined from sources other than the title.

7. U.S. Bureau of the Census, *Historical Statistics of the United States,* 1789–1945 (Washington: Government Printing Office, 1949), 130, series F195.
—Here one group of statistics was cited from among the 25 on page 130.

8. *World Almanac . . . for 1931* (New York: World Telegram and Sun, 1931), 420.
—Here the rule on citing an author or sponsor first is broken. This is such a familiar reference work under its title alone that its identity would be obscured if the editor or publisher were cited first. A dictionary would be a similar exception.

9. *Webster's Third International Dictionary,* "archive."
—This is all you need, and it is so little that the footnote is probably unnecessary. The text might read, "Webster's latest unabridged dictionary defines an *archive* as. . . ."

10. Roy F. Nichols, "The Genealogy of Historical Generalization," in *Generalization in the Writing of History,* ed. by Louis Gottschalk (Chicago: University of Chicago Press, 1963), 130–44.
—A signed article in a book.

Periodicals

The necessary date for locating a periodical does not include place or publisher unless confusion with another periodical would result. What should be included are the following:

1. Author of the article. If it is not signed, but the author is known, bracket his name. If the author is neither given nor known, skip it. Unsigned staff articles in some periodicals are so common that *anonymous* is assumed.

2. Title of the article in quotation marks. Use the title as given at the head of the article, not the one on the cover. Omit title entirely for newspaper articles which carry headlines rather than titles.

3. Title of periodical, underlined in a typescript for printing in italics.

4. Volume and issue numbers when these are helpful. Scholarly and specialized journals, and many older general

magazines, feature these on their covers and are normally bound and cataloged by volume. For this reason, such annotation can help the reader locate them in a library. Separate volume and issue by a colon (24:3) and they will not be confused. Roman numerals have traditionally been used for volume numbers, and you may elect to continue the practice if you see any reason for it. (Quickly: What is XLIX?)

5. Date of issue. Never optional, but if volume and issue have been given, full date follows in parentheses.

6. Page number(s). Not expected for newspaper references, though welcomed by anyone trying to locate an article in a large modern daily.

Examples of First Citations of Periodicals.

1. *Mildred Campbell,* "English Emigration on the Eve of the American Revolution," *American Historical Review* 61:1 (Oct. 1955), 19–20.
2. "The Spirit of '70: Six Historians Reflect on What Ails the American Spirit," *Newsweek,* July 6, 1970, 19–34.
3. Denver *Post,* Nov. 3, 1945.
   —The place of publication is not italicized since it is not considered part of the title.
4. *Rocky Mountain News* (Denver), Nov. 3, 1945.

Published Government Documents

These are books, series, or periodicals which require special attention because identification of sponsors, titles, and parts tends to be complicated, while place of publication need not be specified. When in doubt about a special case, consult either the printed *National Union Catalog: A Cumulative Author List Representing Library of Congress Cards and Titles Submitted by Other American Libraries,* or the Library of Congress printed catalog cards themselves. The *National Union Catalog* is in major libraries, and the printed cards are in most libraries' card catalogs for at least the more recently published works. Here are the standard parts of such citations:

1. Level of government issuing the document: United States (U.S. in footnotes at least), Illinois, Sangamon County, Springfield, or whatever.
    1-A. Agency of the government: Congress, legislature, bureau, board, commission, committee, etc.
    1-B. Division of that agency, as needed, in order of size down to the smallest last. Separate with commas.
2. Title of the work, in italics.
    2-A. Title of the part of the work cited, if any, in quotation marks unless it is only a number or date.
3. Page number(s).

Although many first citations must be rather long, shorter forms may be adapted subsequently. See the section below on Second References: The Short Forms.

Examples of First Citations of Published Government Documents.
1. *Annual Report of the Secretary of State to the Governor of the State of Ohio, for the year ending November 15, 1896,* p. 765.
    —Here all the necessary information appears in the full title. This volume incidentally shows also the importance of taking citations from the title page only: the title given on the spine is "Ohio Statistics, 1896," with the name S. M. Taylor given below. He was the Secretary of State in Ohio that year.
2. U.S. Department of Commerce, Bureau of the Census, *Fourteenth Census of the United States Taken in the Year 1920* (11 vols., Washington, 1922), VI, Part 2: *Agriculture,* 633.
    —The reason for such bureaucratic wordiness is not to impress the reader but to follow library cataloging practices.
3. U.S., Congress, Senate, *Congressional Globe,* 39th Cong., 2d sess., 1867, 39, Pt. 3:1792.
    —This is a reference to a speech reported in one of the predecessors of the *Congressional Record.* The date of the speech may be added parenthetically if you feel it would interest the reader, but it is not an essential finding aid.
4. *Bridges v. California,* 314 U.S. 252 (1941).
    —A U.S. Supreme Court case as usually cited, although the

legal profession and the Government Printing Office omit the italics. Judicial decisions were officially published by private reporting firms for many years, and the citations include their names. For the U.S. Supreme Court, early cases would give the volume, official reporter, and report number thus: 4 Wallace 2. (Or Dallas, Cranch, Wheaton, Peters, or Howard, as the case may be.) For documentation by or for the legal profession, the authority is the latest edition of The Harvard Law Review Association, *A Uniform System of Citation* (Cambridge, Mass.: HLRA).

Unpublished Sources: Manuscripts and Archives

Private letters, diaries, business accounts, and memoranda are typical of the unpublished sources requiring documentation. Their handling is different, but not difficult. You need only to identify the item and its exact location clearly. Information given in the text need not be repeated in the footnote. Thus if you write in the text that your hero wrote a letter to his son John in September 1872, from Seattle, the footnote need only give the exact date of the letter and its present location. Both the place where it was written and the form of the communication—letter, telegram, memo or whatever—are usually indicated unless already understood from the context. Similarly, interview transcripts, diary entries and manuscript memoirs are identified. And if your source was a copy of an original—a carbon, a letterpress copy, a photostat or a film—this should be noted.

Locating the manuscript means answering two obvious questions: to what group or collection does the item belong, and in what institution or ownership? The answers may be simple or otherwise, as in the following examples:

1. Henry Ward Beecher to George Beecher, Dec. 2, 1825, Beecher Papers, Yale University Library.
   —A boyhood letter for which the place is not considered important in the context used. There is only one collection called the Beecher Papers at Yale, and only one Yale University. The abbreviation of names of months with more

than five letters is always proper in footnotes. In all footnotes, a consistent use of a briefer dating style is also usually acceptable. thus: 12/2/25.

2. William T. Crump to The President [Grover Cleveland?]. Jan. 15, 1897; copy in Webb C. Hayes Papers, Hayes Memorial Library, Fremont, Ohio.

3. McKinley to Sarah Duncan, March 18, 1863, in possession of the author.
   —William McKinley is understood from the text; the letter is owned by the author of the book.

4. Author's interview with Marion Butler, Washington, Aug. 7, 1934.

5. James R. Garfield diary entry, Oct. 9, 1901, James R. Garfield Papers, Manuscript Division, Library of Congress.

6. Holmes to Hand, June 24, 1918, Box 103, Folder 24, Learned Hand Papers, Manuscript Division, Harvard Law School Library.
   —Such detailed guidance to box and folder is often needed when a collection is arranged topically rather than chronologically—something to remember when taking notes. In context, the reader will understand that Oliver Wendell Holmes is the writer cited here.

7. Memorandum from Julean Arnold to Far Eastern Section, Nov. 22, 1937, Division of Regional Information, File No. 442.1 General, 1933–44, Bureau of Foreign and Domestic Commerce, RG 151, National Archives.
   —This may not be local history, but it points up the complexity of first citations to massive archives. Fortunately, massive archives are usually administered by experts who can assist researchers with citation problems. "RG" stands for Record Group, which is the basic organizing unit for most modern archives.

Second References: The Short Forms

If the piece you are writing is to include a formal bibliography, then you can safely lean toward the shorter forms in your footnotes from the start, omitting details such as titles of series of volumes, publishers, joint authors, and locations of manuscript collections. These need not be covered twice. But in any case, a source once cited in full should be described in more abbreviated form thereafter. Even if you don't mind repeating long citations, the reader minds reading them, and no publisher wants to pay for the extra type and paper.

There is no rigid formula for acceptable short forms. Commonsense answers will suffice if the right questions are asked: (1) what is needed to assure recognition of the source? (2) what is different about this use of it (page, date, etc.)? (3) what abbreviations should be used for words in repeated use? Whatever you decide, avoid piling on so many abbreviations that an elaborate decoding device is required to unscramble them. Below are some examples of usable short forms of works cited above in full form:

1. Cantor and Schneider, 28.
   —This pair of authors collaborated only on the one book, so there should be no confusion as to title.
2. Thomas, *Portrait for Posterity,* 246.
   —In an article for which only this book by this Thomas was cited, the title could be omitted.
3. Browder [Angstrom], *Reminiscences,* 642.
   —Here the title was shortened and the option was taken to keep both the proper and pen names.
4. *Historical Statistics,* 183, series J101.
   —This is a radical shortening for which the reader should be prepared in advance by a note added to the first citation advising him that the work is "Hereinafter cited as *Historical Statistics.*" Such condensation is only worth the trouble if subsequent citations are fairly frequent.
5. Campbell, "English Emigration," 24.
   —This should be enough to direct the reader to the article. Ellipsis points are not needed to show omissions (as in the case of the shortened title here), since the reader is expected to understand that he is reading a short form.
6. HWB to George Beecher, Dec. 2, 1825, Beecher Papers.
   —If this were a biography of Henry Ward Beecher, the adoption of his initials for all footnote references (except in publication titles) would be an almost necessary economy. Simi-

larly, *Beecher Papers* might be reduced to BP, or to BPY if the collection at Yale must be distinguished from others. Again, however, remember that special abbreviations ought to be explained to the reader before they are adopted, and that too many of them confuses instead of helping.

7. Memo from Julean Arnold to Far Eastern Section, Nov. 23, 1937, Div. Reg. Info. File 442.1, RG 151, NA.

—Sometimes not much shortening is possible. It depends on what you can expect your reader to understand about your sources at the point where you come to the particular citation.

Bibliographies and the Readers' Needs

Your working bibliography was a tool for your own use, prepared early and enlarged as you proceeded in research. It has served its main purpose by the time you have completed your writing. If you choose to add a bibliography to the end of the article or book you are writing, to be presented with it for publication, you are doing something quite different. You are offering the reader a tool for his use.

Now I want to be emphatic. Forget what you may have been asked to give your instructor in a bibliography for a school paper. That was for one reader under special conditions. A publishable bibliography is not an exercise in form or a proof of thoroughness in research. It is solely an aid to the interested reader, and it can be an extremely valuable aid if it is prepared with the same care as the rest of the work. This means making three types of decisions. They have to do with what to include, how to organize, and whether to annotate.

What to include? To begin with, the materials cited in your footnotes are normally listed, but usually some weeding is also necessary. Omit the standard general reference works—dictionaries, almanacs, encyclopedias, and their kin. Also omit materials cited for merely illustrative or incidental purposes, and not generally pertinent to the subject. If, for example, in your preface you quote Thoreau's line about how he had "traveled a good deal in Concord," you may see fit to give a footnote reference, but you have no justification on that basis for listing *Walden* in your bibliography. It would only mystify or annoy your reader.

Trivia and ephemera you have seen in your research should also be weighed for relevance. If you can think of no reason why anyone else should look at an item (even though you did), leave it out. Articles and books which deal with your subject but are flawed with errors or misinterpretations are a different matter. They should be listed and characterized briefly in annotations. Readers appreciate advance warnings of the inadequacies of books they may discover on the library shelves. On the subject of your specialty, you may be the only one who can advise them.

How to organize the list? For up to about fifteen titles, a simple alphabetical list by author's last name should serve the purpose. Any longer list is better classified as to type of source. A simple breakdown into "Books" and "Periodicals" may be enough. More often it is advisable to create additional categories reflecting the wide variety of sources consulted. Here are some typical headings arranged in a suggested order:

> Private Manuscripts and Archives (or simply Manuscripts)
> Personal Interviews and Correspondence
> Published Official Records
> Newspapers
> Secondary Accounts
> Maps, Atlases, and Gazetteers

Additional or substitute headings would be proper in specialized books, the present one included. When the work has a unified theme, the bibliographical sources are customarily listed in groups beginning with the type representing the most personal contemporary material, on the assumption that this is the material closest to the facts. Official records and contemporary newspapers come next. Historical writings of others (secondary accounts) take a still lower place because they are farther from the scene of the action and do not document the facts directly. Listings under each heading are necessarily alphabetized separately.

Should the bibliography be annotated? *Annotation* means adding notes to each of your entries indicating briefly what usefulness they have as sources for your study. Bibliographies in books on history are nearly always more useful when annotated, and it is unfortunate that so few writers take the trouble. True, some entries are almost self-explanatory or may be assumed to be familiar to your readers. These may be left without annotation. But many of your sources have strengths, weaknesses, charms, and eccentricities which you know better than your readers. This is especially true at the time you have just completed writing the text of the work, which is when annotation should be undertaken. Your familiarity with the sources is at its peak, and your insight should be at its sharpest. Some scholarly users may consult your bibliography more closely and frequently than any other part of the book—and judge your work accordingly.

The bibliographical essay is another option one might take in dealing with the organization and annotation of sources. Here the author breaks away from the form of a list and discusses his sources in paragraphs of connected sentences. He can devote an entire paragraph to one major source if he chooses, and another to a group of minor sources. The grouping of types of sources is unchanged, and the formal entries are given in full between parentheses, but the alphabetizing is abandoned in favor of the order dictated by the commentary. Subheadings above paragraphs can clarify the organization of the essay. Consider writing your bibliography in essay style if you feel it might work. You will find it much less like drudgery than list-making, and in fact may enjoy it so much you have to keep editing out your own verbosity.

Bibliographical Entry Forms

The form is the same as for the full citation of a work in a footnote except that if you are alphabetizing, do so by author's last name, name of sponsor, or, lacking those, the first main word of the titles. No reference to page numbers of books is in order; you are citing the whole work now. In the case of newspapers, show the dates of the period for which you examined them (e.g., Springfield *Republican*, 1902–30), except for special cases such as centennial editions or clippings from papers not otherwise examined. (Newspaper clippings in scrapbooks are often from scattered and sometimes unidentified sources. In such cases it may be simplest to list the scrapbook under the original owner's name and then briefly indicate its contents in a note.) If you deliberately omitted any details from your first citations in footnotes (such as a series title covering several volumes), because you thought they could be taken care of in the bibliography, now is the time to take care of them. Finally, there is a preference for setting up the bibliographical entry in a three-part form which gives it a slightly different look from the footnote. Using this approach, the author or sponsor comes first, as usual, but is followed by a period instead of a comma. Then the title(s), followed by another period. Then last the publication data without parentheses, followed by a last period. Thus: Cantor, Norman F., and Richard I. Schneider. *How to Study History.* New York: Crowell, c. 1967. Notice that this sets off the title clearly enough so that if your manuscript is not being prepared for publication and you prefer to keep your page unblackened by frequent underlinings, you may omit underlining the title. For manuals containing extensive samples of bibliographic entries, see the bibliography to this book.

Abbreviations in Documentation

To be recommended, in addition to months, days, and states:

anon.	anonymous
c.	copyright, used only when preceding a date (c. 1948)
ca.	(Latin *circa*) approximately a certain date (ca. 1850). Also written c., but this can be confused with "copyright"
ch. (chs.)	chapter(s)
col. (cols.)	column(s)
comp.	compiler, compiled by

ed.	edition, editor, edited by (when preceding the editor's name)
et al.	(Latin *et alia,* "and others") authors
ibid.	(Latin *ibidem,* "in the same place") referring to an entire work cited in the note immediately preceding
idem	(Latin "the same"). Used in place of author's name in successive references of one note to several works by the same person. Idem is not an abbreviation.
MS (MSS)	manuscript(s), often used to mean "collected papers," as the "Beecher MSS"
n.d.	no date given (for publication of a title)
n.p.	no place, or no publisher, given
p. (pp.)	page(s), when not otherwise clear
rev.	revised, revised by, revision
ser.	series
sic	(Latin "thus") in the sense of "believe it or not!" it may be used sparingly in brackets with a quotation and following an expression or spelling which the reader might interpret as a misprint.
trans., tr.	translated by, translator
vol. (vols.)	volume(s), when not otherwise clear

To be recognized, but not recommended for use:

cf.	confer—but "see" is clearer and equally short as a pointer to another work for comparison or elaboration
f. (ff.)	and the following page(s) or year(s)—legitimate but easily overused.
infra	(Latin "below") Further ahead in the story. "Below" is just as short.
loc. cit.	(Latin *locus citato,* "in the place cited") Used following the author's last name: "Smith, loc. cit." Use the more informative short-title form for footnote references after the first, thus: "Smith, *Lewis County.*" The added type hardly ever requires going over to another line.
op. cit.	(Latin *opera citato,* "in the work cited") Use short-title form, as suggested immediately above.
passim	(Latin "here and there") As a substitute for specific pages in a book, this is so vague that it is usually better omitted. The citation of specific chapters in a book is always ac-

ceptable, and the citation of a title without pages specified implies "here and there."

q.v.   (Latin *quo vide*, "which see") Frequently used for cross references in encyclopedias

supra   (Latin "above") This means that you have already passed it. Say "above."

v., vide   (Latin "see") Say "see," which is shorter and cannot be confused with *versus*

viz.   (Latin *videlicet*, "namely") Quaint

The Process of Writing—and Rewriting

Assuming that you have sketched an outline of the topics you wish to cover, organized your notes for at least the opening sections, and acquainted yourself with the cautions and technicalities discussed in the foregoing sections, it is time to start writing.

You may treat your first draft entirely as a private affair—I do—and especially if it is in longhand, your critics will be glad to wait awhile before reading it. The present book was first drafted in longhand, double spaced, on 8½- by 11-inch ruled paper in a looseleaf notebook. After a section or chapter had been completed in this version, it was typed (with one carbon) by the author. Enough changes were made during this copying process to justify calling the result a second draft. While far from neat, this draft was coherent and legible enough to be shown to others. Changes made at their suggestion or on the author's second thoughts were typed or inked in by the author. The final typing (third draft) was done with greater care for neatness and accuracy. Only then was it submitted to the publisher as a manuscript ready for marking for the printer. The publisher's editor then suggested some further changes and negotiated them with the author. Patches of retyping were called for at this point to insure a manuscript acceptably neat for a printer. At every stage, typing was double-spaced.

The procedure outlined above is not unusual, but neither is it the only right way, except as to the double spacing. There is no right way for everyone. But reviewing the stages in this book's development does illustrate one point which deserves emphasis. This has to do with rewriting.

Rewriting is not a completely separate step. It really includes the application of all those second thoughts and self-criticisms which begin when the first word is crossed out on the first draft. But for practical purposes, it may be treated separately. Rewriting is the period in which the creative intelligence of the writer takes a back seat and the critical mind of the editor begins to drive. To some extent this critical-editorial contribution must come from the author himself. Unless he can detach himself emotionally from his creation, at least to a degree, he cannot respond intelligently to constructive criticisms offered by others. The kind of self-testing that keeps a writer in control of his work at this early stage has been put nicely by George Orwell:

> A scrupulous writer, in every sentence that he writes, will ask himself at least four questions, thus: What am I trying to say? What words will express it? What image or idiom will make it clearer? Is this image fresh enough to have an effect? And he will probably ask himself two more: Could I put it more shortly? Have I said anything that is avoidably ugly?[3]

No amount of revision on your own, however, excuses you from the privileged pain of criticism by an editor. *Every author needs an editor.* The editor's function is to represent the larger readership and speak for it while there is still time for the author to respond constructively. An editor should be someone the author respects, but he need not be any more expert

---

3. "Politics and the English Language," in George Orwell, *A Collection of Essays* (Garden City, N.Y.: Doubleday Anchor ed., 1954), 171. Orwell himself rarely lacked the words to create fresh images. On the same page he says of a propagandist he has quoted: "The writer knows more or less what he wants to say, but an accumulation of stale phrases chokes him like tea leaves blocking a sink."

in the subject matter of the writing than are the readers who will eventually see the finished product. He should be articulate above all, if he is to give constructive help. Teachers, newspapermen, ministers, and occasionally lawyers are prospects worth the local historian's consideration as editors or critics. Lawyers are suggested cautiously because they must read and write so much legal jargon that it is often difficult for them to tune their ears to common idiomatic English. And a sensitive ear for the language is as necessary in an editor as it is in an author. Nothing that sounds awkward (or ugly, as Orwell put it) when spoken is going to read well in print.

Another easily obtainable source of timely help is the book or essay on how to write. Several are recommended in the bibliography, and there are some very good ones to have at hand while you are actually in the throes of making prose.

No amount of advance guidance, however, can replace an editor or make some rewriting unnecessary. An author's ego must be secure enough to withstand an editor's criticism and carry him through the inevitable negotiations calmly. Knowing that every other essay on how to write has itself been revised and rewritten has been some consolation to the present writer, never more so than while following an editor's advice to insert the paragraph you are just finishing reading.

The Prepared Manuscript

The look of a manuscript that is ready for a printer or publisher will depend finally on whether it is to be printed from photographic images of the typescript. If it is, you or somebody must prepare camera-ready copy. This means typing each page just as you want it to appear in all respects but page and illustration size, which can be reduced if you wish. Margins and other spacings are crucial, and all typographical errors must be cleaned up without a visible trace on the manuscript. Illustrations must be placed correctly. See the section on direct image composition in the following chapter for more on how to proceed in this direction.

If it is to be set in printer's type, a manuscript should be typed double spaced throughout in the same size of type (pica or elite) and with regular margins. Irregularities in any of these matters cause problems in estimating length. Minor corrections are no problem if they are made neatly. Directions to the printer as to typefaces and spacing must also be provided eventually, but these matters should await consultation with the printer or publisher. He will mark the pages in a code language of technical abbreviations you have no need to learn.

Below is a checklist of the usual parts of a book, given in order from front cover to index. Such outward trimmings as a dust jacket or slip case are omitted as seldom applicable. The checklist:

A. Cover design
B. Half title
C. Title page
D. Copyright notice
E. Catalog information and ISBN entry
F. Table of contents
G. List of illustrations
H. Foreword
I. Preface
J. Acknowledgments
K. List of abbreviations
L. Text
M. Appendix
N. Source notes
O. Bibliography
P. Index

Not every book needs every one of these parts, but it is well to think ahead and decide which are appropriate. The following are some explanatory notes and suggestions on each item in the list.

A. *Cover.* The wording for this should be carefully determined and typed on a separate sheet marked "cover text." Design ideas, including any artwork, should be noted separately and discussed with your printer or publisher. For suggestions on cover design and construction, see the sections on design considerations and binding in the following chapter.

B. *Half title.* This is an unnumbered right-hand page giving the title of the book, either alone or with an acknowledgment to a sponsoring organization or a statement of the title of the series to which the volume belongs. Frequently this page is not really needed. It might be a candidate for elimination if the final layout of pages for printing shows that paper costs would be affected.

C. *Title page.* Here are the full title, the author's name, the publisher's name, and the place (with usually the year) of publication. Embellishments on the author's name—titles, degrees, etc.—are out of fashion. Give your name as you would sign a check, or as you would want it on your tombstone. If the work is an edited document, the author's name should be supplemented by whatever is appropriate: "Edited by ———" "Compiled by ———" or "Translated by ———." If the author is also the publisher, wording such as "Printed for the author by [name of printing firm]" is in order, followed by place and date as usual.

D. *Copyright notice.* The standard location for this is on the reverse of a book's title page. The form is simple, but be sure that the year given is that of the first publication of a new book. This notice must be printed if a copyright is to be valid. Be sure to follow through with an application to the Copyright Office in Washington if you are serious about your claim to statutory protection. A letter requesting an application should go to The Register of Copyrights, Library of Congress, Washington, D.C. 20025.

E. *Catalog information and ISBN entry.* These are best included just above the copyright notice. A Library of Congress Catalog Card Number may be obtained through an inquiry to the Processing Division, Library of Congress, Washington, D.C. 20540. An International Standard Book Number may be assigned by the ISBN Agency, R. R. Bowker Company, 1180

Avenue of the Americas, New York, N.Y. 10036, to which inquiries should be addressed. ISBNs are always the publisher's responsibility rather than the author's. If you are privately publishing a single book primarily for local distribution, an ISBN will not be of value to you. Its purpose is to expedite inventory controls and ordering through computers.

F. *Table of contents.* This is usually labeled simply "Contents" on the page itself. It may be put together (except for page numbers) before page proofs are received and accepted. In the case of a work to be printed directly from the image on the typed page, even the numbers should be inserted. It was once customary to place this page just before the beginning of the text, but the trend now is toward moving it toward the front of the front matter (items A-K in the list here) to make it more easily accessible.

G. *List of illustrations.* This is a specialized table of contents, and need not start on a new page. It may give the captions of pictures in summary form. If all the illustrations are grouped together on consecutive, unnumbered pages, a simple direction to the numbered page just preceding the group is all that is needed.

H. *Foreword.* Note the spelling: this is a "word before," not "Forward," a call to attack. It is an introductory essay like a preface but written by someone else and normally signed at the end, perhaps with his title added if that helps explain his appearance. If, for example, you have completed a history of your city and would like to have the current mayor contribute some introductory remarks, this is the place.

I. *Preface.* Here the author first addresses himself to the reader if he wishes, and has his first opportunity to justify his book. He may wish to explain how it came to be written, what contribution he hopes it makes, and what limitations of scope or adequacy he feels it has. If both are brief, the acknowledgments may be made a concluding section of the preface without a separate heading.

J. *Acknowledgments.* These may be grouped under a separate heading on a new page if desired, or squeezed in less prominently. Included, of course, should be specific acknowledgments of permission to quote, especially from copyrighted works. Equally important are the brief notes thanking by name those who gave you substantial help along the way from research through publication.

K. *List of abbreviations.* This is seldom needed, but a good place for it is on the left-hand page just preceding page 1 of the text.

L. *Text.* Here begins page 1 of the arabic numerals to be carried through to the last page of the index. All pages ahead of this one should be numbered in small roman numerals consecutively from the title page, although the numerals are not usually printed until the first page of the foreword, which is numbered on a right-hand page and after that only on pages that have no main heading or title at the top.

M. *Appendix.* One or several appendices may be useful for segregating long notes, documents, tables, or charts which are important for reference but cannot be fitted smoothly into the main text. Each appendix deserves a number or letter and explanatory title, and a notation in the table of contents. Pagination normally is continued from the text itself.

N. *Source notes* (or Notes on Sources, or Reference Notes, or just Notes). Explanatory notes should be kept as footnotes at the bottom of the pages of text, but reference footnotes are increasingly becoming backnotes. Regardless of the final placement of "footnotes" of every description, in the final copy prepared for the printer they should be typed double-spaced on separate sheets of paper with headings and pagination separate for each chapter. The printer will set this material in a smaller type at a different time and then relocate it as directed. Again, text typed for direct photographic reproduction is an exception. Decisions as to the placement and spacing of these source notes must be made before final typing begins, since "what you see is what you get" when the typed page is printed by this process.

O. *Bibliography.* This has been discussed above. It is frequently and usually more accurately called something else—Selected Bibliography, For Further Reading, or Bibliographical Note.

P. *Index.* Every book-length work of history ought to have enough reference value to deserve a good index. To prepare one for a typeset book, the author must await the arrival of final page proofs. It has not seemed worth the extensive space it would require to take up the problems of indexing here, but guidance is available in The University of Chicago Press *Manual of Style* (which gives thirty pages to the subject), Sherman Kent's *Writing History* (twenty pages), or Martha T. Wheeler's *Indexing,* all listed in the Bibliography.

A Word on Illustrations

Illustrations and related graphic work are too often considered wholly apart from writing, as afterthoughts or decorations. Yet illustrations can only be presented to fullest advantage if the writer is contantly alert to his responsibility for them—and their possibilities for him. They may be referred to pointedly in descriptive passages, character sketches, and itineraries. They should reinforce the written words, and can sometimes communicate better than words alone.

Watch your fellow browsers in a bookstore some time. Notice how often they look at a book's cover first (necessarily), open it to glance at its title page, scan its table of contents, and then flip through to the pictures, pausing over a few of them before setting the book down again. First impressions are persistent, and when they are unfavorable they may not be followed by any further impressions at all. Because your captions are associated with your illustrations, and so will be read by more people than your text, they, too, deserve special handling. They should document the sources (remember those credit lines!), creators, forms, and subjects of the illustrations.

Good pictures and maps are not necessarily the added expense in bookmaking they once were, thanks to new technology. They are still not free, but neither is a page of words. Technical considerations in designing and printing them are discussed later under the appropriate headings.

A Tip on Mailing

You do not need to pay first-class postage when sending a book manuscript or an article if you can allow a few days for its delivery. Mark the envelope or box "Special Fourth-Class Rate—Manuscript" and pay only the going rate for that class. If you enclose a letter, note also "Letter Enclosed" and add first-class postage only for the letter. Material sent at the special rate may be sealed and insured. There is a seventy-pound limit on packages at the special rate, but that presents a problem only to a very few of our deepest thinkers in the historical profession.

Editing Documents for Publication

Every historian probably feels at some time that the most valuable contribution he can make to historical scholarship at that moment is to put an especially interesting document into print where it can receive the attention it deserves. A single document rarely takes much editing effort for the scholar familiar with its context. A major collection, of course, can require a large part of his career. Clarence E. Carter was perhaps the first American to make a distinguished career in historical editing, and he left eighteen volumes of *The Territorial Papers of the United States* (Washington, 1934–52) to show for it. Over the past two decades, scholars working on the papers of several presidents have followed the lead of Julian P. Boyd, editor of *The Papers of Thomas Jefferson* (Princeton, 18 vol.s, 1950–71, still incomplete) in developing a highly refined and demanding editorial procedure for their work. Their sometimes extreme detail in annotation and explanation, however, is not likely to be imitated by anyone with limited time and funds, nor need it be. A case can be made for comparing historical editing to restoring antique furniture: repair and refinishing should not be carried to the point where the result looks "better than new" and just as lacking in mystery or charm. This is not the place to argue the matter at length, but

I am convinced that there are shorter paths to useful documentary publication than those followed by the recent editors of the monumental editions of presidential papers.

Whether you have one document or a great many under consideration, the basic problems are the same. They concern the relevance and coherence of the material. Relevance here means some significant connections to other material on the same subject. Coherence means a reasonable degree of focus and clarity in communicating. Your job as editor is to find these two qualities in the material and emphasize them. You help the reader see what you have seen and found worthwhile.

For a hypothetical example, you have a Civil War soldier's diary covering most of two years and running about 4,500 words in length. You know there are thousands of soldier diaries still unpublished since 1865, and you have read enough of them to know most of their common features. This one has several peculiarities which you note for attention in your introduction: perhaps his assignment to field hospital duty, his encounter with General Butler, his narration of a foraging and looting expedition, and his impressions of New Orleans under occupation. These are given special attention, perhaps along with a few other topics such as evidence on his attitudes on the aims of the war, toward his enemy, and toward his folks at home. You try to learn something from other sources about his pre-war background and his military and postwar career. Some of this information is used in the introduction, some in footnotes (the identification of Butler, for example), and some in a postscript. Dull stretches of the diary may be omitted in favor of brief summaries of their content in your own words. The punctuation, spelling, and capitalization of the diarist are irregular but you decide to leave them alone. You insert missing words in brackets where needed for clarity. Then you try out your edited result on a few friends to see if they feel you have added or omitted too much. Finally, having had a neatly typed copy prepared, you send it to the journal of your state historical society (or to *Civil War History*) and hope for the best. You can expect them to take awhile in evaluating, questioning, and the rest, but if you have done your homework and are patient, and if the length is not excessive for the publication you have chosen, your chances of seeing your document in print are good.

Diaries and journals are sometimes long enough to justify their publication in book form, and there are many examples of the loving editorial care which can give almost ordinary documents an extraordinary dramatic life and depth of meaning. I will limit examples to one personal favorite, *Trail to California: The Overland Journal of Vincent Geiger and Wakeman Bryarly,* edited with an introduction by David M. Potter (New Haven: Yale University Press, 1945, paperback edition 1962). After warming up with a preface and a map, Potter takes 73 pages and 197 footnotes to get through his introduction, provides headnotes and footnotes for the 136 pages of the journal, and concludes with four short appendices, an annotated bibliography, and an index. The very weight of such trappings might make a lively narrative seem dull, but in this case it has the opposite effect because Professor Potter, for all his scholarship, was himself never dull. His additions were profuse but always pertinent to the questions of relevance and coherence.

Such lavish care tends to transform the document into the editor's own book, and cannot be recommended as a generally useful standard for that reason. Yet anyone facing the challenge of historical editing can study the work of Potter and the editors of the Presidential Papers with profit. If their approach is perhaps overly detailed, their execution is exemplary.

A collection of letters or other writings may be approached in basically the same way as a diary. Each letter in a series is comparable to an entry in a diary. Some may be shortened or omitted in favor of summaries as long as the reader is told when such breaks occur. Having all of your words as editor underlined for printing in italics helps keep that distinction. Some letters may be entirely omitted without further ado if they seem to dilute the series with trivia. Leaving an item unpublished is not the same as throwing it away, and presumably the originals will be preserved.

With a series of letters it is often space-saving for you and helpful to the reader if a headnote is provided above each letter. A consistent form for the series ought to be adopted, and it should include (1) the names and locations of the writer and recipient as fully as the reader will need, (2) the date, as far as it is known, with the editor's additions inserted in brackets, (3) the exact present location of the original if different from the others, and (4) any new information helpful in understanding the tone or content of the letter. Thus, if you know that the writer is a cousin who owes the recipient money for a reason you understand but the letter leaves obscure, you have material for a helpful note.

Explanatory notes are always a matter of judgment. What is to be explained and whether anyone is likely to want it explained are perennial questions. Publishers and their editors can be helpful in some cases, but primarily your guide must be your own feel for the interests and background of your readers. As a matter of practical economics, try to keep footnotes to a minimum. It will frequently suffice to put all explanations in the headnote above a short document, with bracketed words or phrases inserted in the text where clarification is needed. Either of these devices is less interruptive than a footnote.

Reprinting in a New Edition

Up to this point, historical editing has been treated as something one does to previously unpublished work. Reprinting a scarce book of continuing value, however, calls for the same general approach. Suppose you find a rare copy of the first history of your county. It is in reasonably good condition, but on thorough inquiry you can locate only a few copies, and you note that the last time a dealer in rare books offered one for sale he mentioned its scarcity and asked $120 for it. Then you ask yourself whether the book is still useful as history. In spite of omissions, errors, and oddities, does it still offer something no later work offers? If several local historians agree that the answer is affirmative, you might explore the market for a reprint.

Since the book has already been printed once, the new edition might well be done as a photo-offset facsimile of the pages of the original edition. New material would be confined to a separately paged introduction and a revised title page identifying the new edition, sponsor, and date. You may copyright your new material, but not the old. And if the original book was published since 1905, stop everything and check its copyright status. (On copyrights, see pp. 75-77.)

Taking responsibility for reviving a book does normally call for some explanation on your part, and this is the main purpose of a new introduction. It is like writing a thoughtful but favorable book review. It would be a disservice to new readers to omit it.

In some cases it may also be important to add explanatory or critical notes at various points in the original text. Without changing a word, you can correct errors and supply new material briefly by inserting footnotes on pages you are resetting in new type, or in backnotes if you are not resetting. An index, if one was lacking in the original, would also be a welcome feature of the new edition. If the original did include an index, remember that in order for it to remain valid now there must be no changes in pagination.

A Note on Translations

In some parts of the country, great quantities of the most important documents of the early period are virtually locked up in their foreign languages. All New York historians talk about the Dutch, but very few read Dutch. Mississippi Valley French is a similar problem, German extends from the east coast to St. Louis and Milwaukee, and Spanish pervades the documentation of the southwestern communities. There are not nearly enough historians capable or patient enough to deal with the problem directly. What they can do in some cases is to search out and encourage those nonhistorians who could help. Collaboration between those who can deal with the language and those who can deal with the historical setting is teamwork both can enjoy and gain from. Each can share the other's enthusiasm once a start is made. My plea here is for local historians to make the start.

CHAPTER THREE

Publishing

MANUSCRIPTS are written; books are published. The only manuscripts that become books are those that attract the capital and skills necessary to see them through the publication process. It is the same as in the theater, where the script of a play becomes a staged production only after it has found a producer capable of rounding up the funds and talents needed to bring the playwright's work to an opening night audience. Though a published book requires no actors to speak its lines, it does need an editor who functions very much as a play director; it calls on designers, accountants, and advertising and marketing specialists as well as printers and binders.

Note that publishing is a much broader term than printing. Publishing is "making public," and printing is only one step in that long process. Publishing firms do not normally have printing plants of their own, and printing firms do not publish.

There are three basic types of publishers, two of them in business mainly for profit and one mainly for the service it can provide. The familiar names are the large commercial firms—Harper and Row, McGraw-Hill, Random House, Knopf, Macmillan, Norton, Viking, and others. Each of them is more or less subdivided, department-store fashion, into divisions according to markets (juveniles, college, school texts, trade books, etc.) and typically they depend heavily on literary agents for sources of manuscripts. There are directories of book and magazine publishers, as well as a quantity of advice on their interests and habits, in several of the books listed in the bibliography.

A second commercial type of firm is the only type to solicit manuscripts by advertising for them. Often referred to as vanity presses, these firms operate with less capital and risk because they normally require their authors to put up some or all of the direct costs of publication. Such an arrangement is proper enough and doubtless meets a need. Every type of publisher accepts subsidies in special cases. But unless a publisher carries some of the risk on a book's success, he cannot be expected to exercise much effort or independent judgment in its behalf.

The third type comprises the nonprofit university or institutional presses. Their special strength is in reaching the market for scholarly books, and it is for their service to scholarship (and the prestige of the activity, perhaps) that they are supported by educational institutions. Many of them are quite conscious of the region they are located in, a fact to be considered by local historians looking for a friendly reception. While they are more patient about realizing a return on a book and will normally keep it in print while any hope for it lasts, university presses are not eager to lose money. Do not expect them to risk more than breaking even, or to neglect an opportunity to return a profit to the author and themselves. They are nonprofit only in the sense that they do not have shareholders looking for dividends. They can and do make profits on some transactions, but the money is used to maintain or expand the operation. In recent decades this type of press has been encouraged to the point where there are at least one major and several smaller university presses in every region of the country. Similar to them in operation but usually narrower in purpose are the publishing facilities of the religious denominations and a few foundations and research institutions. Some historical agencies also publish books as well as journals, and have produced some work of real excellence. You should acquaint yourself with the situation in your own state. If you have a manuscript on a subject of interest to it, your state historical agency might at the least be a source of useful suggestions leading toward publication. Too frequently they are themselves the logical publishers in every respect but one: they lack funds.

All of the above considerations have to do with professional publishers. Often local history cannot attract professional involvement because the interest and potential market seems too small to justify the necessary investment even if the manuscript is competently prepared. This has happened a thousand times before, and there is a solution to it. You do it yourself, or get your interested friends to join you in doing it. This is amateur, or what is usually called private publication. The author, the organization sponsoring his work (a museum, historical society, church, club, or business), or a combination of them, takes direct responsibility for the book's costs, arranging for design, printing contracts, editing and proofing, and promotion and sales. Taken as a whole, it is too much for one person to manage, but a sensible delegation of jobs within a relatively small group of dedicated and cooperative citizens can succeed very well and they can have some fun in the process. Just how the work should be shared is a matter of local option. There is no responsibility necessarily fixed on the author himself beyond that of proofreading. Layout and design may be treated separately or may be handled by the person who selects and deals with the printer. Advertising, sales, and financial accounting may each be delegated separately under a business manager chosen to coordinate their efforts. Advance subscriptions may be solicited, perhaps at a discounted price (once the right price has been determined), and that campaign may be one person's special assignment. The notes and suggestions that follow will deal primarily with the various jobs themselves, rather than the question of how they should be allocated. For the author who has found a publisher, the rest of this chapter may help him to understand what he is getting in services and talents, and remind him to count his blessings.

Design Considerations

This section might well be read twice: once before making up printing specifications and again afterward, especially if the printers all estimate more than you feel can or should be spent. Design never takes place in an economic vacuum. At the same time, certain design choices must be considered before the printer can get a clear picture of what you want from him.

Every book is designed; there is no escaping it. To be indifferent to the whole matter is to guarantee a homely, awkward-looking book. Printers are not paid to be designers, and although they can be extremely helpful they should not be held responsible for their customers' ineptness. To take care in design from the start is certain to improve the readability and attractiveness of the result even if the budget finally dictates some compromises with perfection.

Forget the budget for a moment: how do you really want your book to look? After you have fixed your ideal book in mind you can begin to find out where your taste is too expensive or impractical and where your hopes can be realized with no additional expense at all. In any case, *too expensive* is a relative term. Some books are too expensive because they are too cheaply produced. That is, they remain unsold at a low price because prospective buyers are looking for a higher level of quality, and buy only when they find it. The right price is not necessarily the lowest one.

Think about the outside first. There is little point in repeating "you can't judge a book by its cover"; it is done all the time and can't be helped. If you are near your own bookshelf at the moment (or in a bookstore or library, reading this free), look at some covers. What do they tell you about the character of the contents, about the taste of the publisher, and about the buying public the books were designed to attract? Here are some types you may recognize:

1. The paperback mystery or novel from the drugstore. Its cover is aggresively dramatic, vivid enough to catch your eye

and encourage your impulse to give it a fling for ninety-five cents. It invites a brief flirtation, with no expectation that you will take it home to Mother or ask it to join the family forever.

2. The official government report, the law book or biographical dictionary. Typically these are strictly business. They have their names plainly stamped on their rigid hard-cover spines and seem to say, "I am reliable, durable, useful, and respectable, but don't expect a thrill a minute."

3. The coffee table book, or gift book, heavy under a glossy cover which illustrates a popular theme from history, the arts, or travel. It bespeaks the elegant host inviting you for a stroll through a gallery or museum, with some paragraphs of commentary along the way.

And so on, each book almost as individual on its face as it is inside, but making the same strong first impression that human faces do. This is why it is so important in designing to choose colors, materials, lettering, and artwork consistent with the overall character and purpose of the contents inside. Assuming that you have a manuscript of a serious book intended for lasting appeal and dignified company on a library or living room bookshelf, here are some suggestions. They apply equally to thin pamphlets and bulky tomes.

1. Avoid a cover that is crowded or gaudy in appearance. The front page of a tabloid newspaper is not a model to follow. In fact, any lettering that looks like newspaper headlines will detract, if only subconsciously, from the prospective reader's confidence in the book.

2. Avoid amateur artwork anywhere in the book, but especially on the cover. The slightest clumsiness will attract all the attention, and no explanations will help.

3. Be cautious about designs that are intended to suggest the historic past. If the time period or location of the art you have available are not entirely appropriate to the story inside, settle for some well-chosen lettering.

4. Hard covers may be printed separately from the

pages on different presses and by different firms. Lithographers are capable of reproducing nearly any image on nearly any surface you want—a photograph on linen-weave cloth, for example, if you need it.

5. Make the most of each color you pay for, starting with the cover stock itself, and the first ink applied to it, which can be used both at part strength (screened) and full. A second ink allows up to four additional color effects (full over the cover, screened over the cover, full and screened over the first ink). But don't take risks with subtle combinations you or your printer have never actually seen produced *with the inks and cover stock in question.* When it comes to colors in printing, you can only afford to believe what you see.

Display Types

One or two typefaces in various sizes are needed for the headings from the cover through the title page, part, chapter, and section headings. These are the display types. They may be chosen either before or after the type for the text, but in any case should relate to it either in close harmony or clear contrast. The title page needs only three elements: title, author, and publisher, in that order from the top of the page. In general, look at what is done in books similar to yours, see if you can get Marshall Lee's *Bookmaking* and study pages 86–95 for ideas, and by all means consult with your printer before fixing too firmly on your selections. A printer's experience and taste may not help you to find the best possible choices, but they will protect you from some of the worst. Equally important, you must finally settle on typefaces and sizes that your printer has available.

Most printers who set type (do composition) have a booklet displaying the typefaces in their stock, with at least one-line samples of each and notations on other sizes available. Ask your printer whether he also buys composition from another firm specializing in typesetting, and if he does you can widen your choices with another sample book. There may be no added cost to you. You may find, in fact, that the printer who gives you the lowest price turns out to be one who buys all his composition from others. Such a subcontracting arrangement need not concern you if you have seen that your printer has obtained satisfactory results from it in the past.

A Typeface for the Text

Choosing a typeface for the main text of your work is important but not difficult. Every printer has at least one typeface adequate to your needs, and some have a bewildering variety. The important thing is to know what your needs are. There is room for individual taste and style here, although definite boundaries are set by the need for high readability. I would go so far as to urge you not to aim for beauty in choosing how you want your pages of text to look. Aim instead at two other qualities—a character of type consistent with the character of the book, and high readability—and you will come closer to beauty than if you were to go at it directly. The same advice goes for choosing paper.

The most traditional and familiar letter forms belong to the family of roman faces. Since history is a traditional form of literature and takes the past for its subject matter, there is perhaps a special appropriateness to a roman typeface for printing it. The effect need not be one of quaintness—newspapers and popular magazines use the same faces—but neither will it allow your book to take on the look of a computer print-out or business report. Novelty has its place in display types and advertising, where only a few words are seen together, but the single most important contributor to readability of a type set in paragraphs and pages (sizes, lengths of lines and colors being the same) is simple familiarity. This has always been true, and explains the slowness of change in letter forms. The *Reader's Digest,* for example, is set in Granjon, a Linotype face almost indistinguishable from the original letters first cut in that style in France in the mid-sixteenth century. (The *Digest's* display type, Frye's Baskerville, is more daring. It is based on a late eighteenth-century model.) Among the other traditional faces that one could feel equally safe in considering are Bembo, Caledonia, Garamond (or the Garamont variety), Janson, Scotch Roman, Times Roman, and the relatively new Palatino.

Besides the style of face, there are three other decisions to be made in the interests of readability—and because your printer needs to know; these are *size, leading,* and *measure.* Size refers to the height of the type as printed, and it is noted in *points* (about 1/72 of an inch). Lead (pronounced "ledd," after the metal) refers to the amount of white space opened between the lines. Type that is set in 8-point on 8-points (expressed as 8/8), as newspapers have traditionally been, is said to be set solid; if set 8 on 9, or 8/9, it is leaded one point. Books are frequently set 10 on 12, and this may be taken as a conservative or economical norm. Some typefaces require more leading and a larger size than others for equivalent readability. This notably true of Bembo, which is practical for book texts only at a minimum 12/13 size.

The third decision affecting readability (and costs) is on the measure, or length of the line of type. There is no absolute rule about it, but the consensus seems to be that readability begins to fall off when a line goes beyond about 60 characters, including spaces, of closely spaced lines. The problem is evident to anyone reading a page full of single-spaced typewriting—typewriters are usually set for 70 characters per line. Double spacing on a typewriter has the same good effect that leading does on printed type. The extra space between lines helps the reader locate the start of each new line as he scans back from the right-hand end of the previous line. The longer the line, the more leading needed.

The book you are now reading is set in 11/13 Baskerville (Mergenthaler VIP), set 26 picas wide (*pica* is a printer's measure; there are about six to the inch). All these measures might have been different had another page size been chosen. Page margins vary according to taste and cost requirements, except that the inside margin should not be much less than ¾ inch.

The Right Paper

Getting the right paper for your book may be the most unappreciated achievement in the process of book designing. Getting the wrong paper, on the other hand, can attract attention all too easily—by reflecting a blinding glare that hides the print, by showing ink through the pages, or by blotting and blurring illustrations, all, as likely as not, without saving money.

This is not the kind of attention you are looking for. You can avoid it by giving attention to its sources. Real expertise in the huge and complex business of paper engineering and management is a lifetime undertaking. But if you have a reliable printer and some idea of what to ask for and what to avoid, you have a very good chance of getting the right paper and hearing no more about it.

Only a few of the many characteristics of book papers need concern you directly; the rest the printer can deal with. You should be able to borrow booklets of sample swatches of various papers from a printer, or to obtain them free from a paper wholesaler by a phone call or letter. You need not have the actual prices at first; they are too complex to be intelligible, and in any case your printer will have to do the actual estimating and ordering. Relative costs are discussed in an introductory way below, and you can carry on from there with more recent and local advice. Paper technology is improving every year. There have been significant improvements in the early 1970s in the quality and versatility of papers partly or entirely of recycled material. Use them when you can. It should cost you little or nothing and you will spare a few trees.

Now for some notes on specific paper characteristics as they affect design.

Bulk. Would you like your publication to be fatter without being heavier, so that its 64 pages look like 88 or more? Or would you prefer the slimmest booklet you can get, perhaps because you plan to bind with wire-stitching and don't want the pages to spring open? The rough-surfaced antique finishes are especially high-bulking, but are neither heavier nor costlier than the machine-finish smoother papers.

Opacity. The antique papers have somewhat greater opacity for their weight than smoother finishes. If dark or contrasty illustrations or any photographs are to be used, take special care to obtain the weight of paper needed to prevent show-through. Text paper of a weight called "70 pound" may be necessary for the purpose, but opacity is not a matter on which to compromise. Otherwise well-designed books have been ruined in appearance because show-through made every page look dirty. This book is printed on 60–pound stock.

Suitability for Illustrations. Line drawings, outline maps, and some photographs (those not requiring much detail for effectiveness) will reproduce on antique papers. Smoother papers will bring out finer detail and tonal gradations in photographs and other halftones. As you go from uncoated to pigmented to dull-coated papers you get sharper results, although costs increase somewhat at the same time. Glossy-coated papers are also made, but their distracting glare is a nuisance in books.

Color. White papers include some varieties of such cold, almost florescent brightness that they tire the eyes after a while. But if you are using full-color illustrations you will want a bright white for best results. As a background for print alone, warmer tints are more comfortable. A pronounced color tint that calls attention to itself is a poor choice for a long book, besides being expensive. In any case, tinted paper must be considered as part of the color scheme. How will it affect halftone illustrations? Will it work to advantage with a colored ink?

Endpapers. Books bound in hard covers are glued to their bindings partly by a heavy endpaper made for the purpose. The choice of this paper is important to a book's design because one leaf is conspicuous in front of the first printed page and two of the leaves determine the color of the insides of the covers. At little extra expense you can have some choices of color and texture. A harmony or contrast with the cover is the most obvious choice—blue cover with red or light blue end leaves, yellow cover with tan or dark green end leaves, and so on. But beware of combinations of black and red unless you want your book to be mistaken for a Bible.

Cover Papers. Thanks to the popularity of paperback books over the last generation, there is a wide choice of soft-cover materials. How much wear do you expect your cover will need to take? You can get covers that will outlast your children's use for nearly anything except feeding the furnace. What kind of printing or artwork do you want? You can get nearly any kind without sacrificing durability. The most durable covers are impregnated or coated with plastic, and some have the texture of cloth. When you see what looks right in the sample book, check with your printer on its cost and suitability.

Hard Covers. Durability should be an important concern if you are paying for hard covers. Unfortunately, you cannot assume that high quality goes with the added expense; there are cloths that both give and show stains, and especially if the book has no dust jacket these must be avoided.

Halftone artwork is possible on cloth, as you can see from school textbook covers. This is a separate operation and expense, however. For a small edition, it is more common to limit the design to die-stamped titling. The die stamp also costs extra, but not much in relation to the total binding costs. What you get is a distinctive bite of the design into the cloth, a durable as well as attractive feature. Metallic foils are frequently used—gold, silver, and bronze especially. The typeface for the die stamp should not be too small or have delicate hairlines or fine serifs, since even a good die cannot stand very much pounding without showing wear. Separate dies are made for stamping the spine and the front cover. If the front cover design is spread out, it may also require more than one die.

A *blind stamp* is one that carries no ink or foil. As a subordinate design element it can be an effective decoration. A monogram, signature, or simple pictorial design may be impressed clearly enough to be seen and felt without competing with the title and author for attention.

Printing on cloth covers is also done by offset, conventional letterpress, and by silk-screening. The latter process uses a highly opaque paint which can be essential if a light color is to be printed over a dark cover stock in one run through the press.

Illustrations

Strictly from a design standpoint, illustrations seldom present major problems. If they have been carefully selected, captioned, integrated with the text where appropriate, and given the right paper and press for printing, they cannot fail too badly. With modern-day offset printing, almost any illustration can be printed on almost any paper, although a smoother paper helps for fine halftones. With letterpress printing, a smooth paper is necessary for photographs and very fine line drawings. Room for improvement is usually in the areas of placement, scaling, and cropping, which are discussed below. Final decisions on these matters can be held until galley proofs are available and the pages are being made up.

In placing illustrations, begin with those so closely related to the text that they require a specific page location to be effective. Those remaining may be spread out to obtain a more even balance. Unfilled pages at the ends of chapters may be used. But avoid placing illustrations at only one or two of a series of formal dividing points such as chapter headings; this can cause confusion.

Locating illustrations on the page is a matter of exercising taste within the limits of the printing method to be used. If you are using letterpress, it is most economical to keep the illustrations within the same page margins as the text. At least a ¼-inch margin is needed because the frame (called a chase) in which metal type is locked requires this much to hold the tightening devices.

Photo-offset printing allows for the extension of a picture to any or all edges of a page. The only hitch is that you must allow ⅛-inch at each edge for the knife that trims the pages. If the picture is to be cropped at the edge of the page anyway, the printer can confine his trimming to the cropped portion if so directed. To make your wants known, you need the term *bleed* in your vocabulary. A picture which is printed to the edge of a page is said to bleed. So, for example, if you crop a picture top and right and want it to bleed top and right as well, note on the back (and on the page layout or dummy also) that you want it printed, say "5 inches wide + bleed." If you have not cropped, but still want to go to the edge, a little cropping will be done by the knife in order to make sure the illustration bleeds. Printers are not sadistic in this; they assume you don't want to see a thin sliver of white paper at the edges.

Sometimes it is necessary to spread an illustration across two facing pages. Printers can accomplish this, but the exact alignment of the two halves is difficult. A double-page spread is easily managed, however, if it appears on pages adjoining in the middle of a *signature* (a gathering of pages folded as a unit). Here the two pages are one piece of paper, and no alignment problem arises. If you need a large map, for example, and can choose where to locate it, let it have pages 8–9 of a 16-page signature, or 16–17 of a 32-page signature. If you are not certain of how the signatures will be gathered in your book, ask the printer. He wants to avoid alignment problems as much as you do.

Scaling. How much enlargement or reduction will each illustration accept without losing detail or taking on an unattractive texture? Simple woodcuts are often intended to be kept small and will appear crude or blotchy when enlarged. Subtly shaded halftones—photographs especially—and detailed maps need ample room. If you have lettering in an illustration, you must decide whether the legibility of the words is important.

The Process of Scaling. Suppose you have a picture 7 inches deep and 9 inches wide, and want it reduced to 5 inches in width. How deep will it be? There are three ways to find out. One is with a proportional scale, which looks like a slide rule and may be bought at a drafting supplies store. (Get one measured in inches.) A second is with simple algebra: $7/9 =$

x/5, which is cross-multiplied to get $9x=35$, which makes $x =$ $35 \div 9$, or just under 4.

The third method is with geometry, and it has the advantage of giving a visual result. The principle is that similar rectangles have the same diagonal. So you can take a clean sheet of paper and mark off a rectangle 7 inches by 9 inches, using the edges of the sheet for two of the sides to save time. Then draw a diagonal within the rectangle, from corner to corner. Next make a new line showing the width reduced to 5 inches. Where it crosses the diagonal, you have the point marking your reduced depth, so measure it and you have your answer. If you measure again up the other side the same distance and draw the line of your new side, you will have an outline of your reduced picture.

To enlarge your original, extend the diagonal of the original out until it crosses the line marking the new width. At that point you have reached the new depth. In the illustration on

Scaling Geometrically

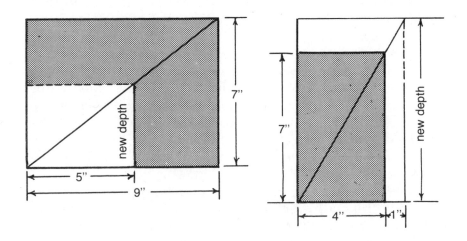

The shaded rectangles represent the original sizes in both cases

the right below, the original is 7 inches by 4 inches and the aim is to see what happens when the width is enlarged an inch, to 5 inches. In the case of the enlargement, your new depth is 8¾ inches. If your page size is too small to carry that much, you have a problem; if your maximum depth allowed is 8 inches, then you may measure up just 1 inch from the original 7 inches, run the new top line across and see how much width that adds. It will meet the diagonal at a width of 4 4/7 inches. (Mark it 4½ inches for the printer.) If you insist on the full 5 inch width, you must change the proportions of the picture by marking some of the top or bottom (or both) for masking out in printing. In the case above, the original 7 inches by 4 inches would have to be cut down to 6 2/5 inches by 4 inches to enlarge to 8 inches by 5 inches. This kind of trimming is called cropping, and is discussed below. Before going on to it, however, two notes of caution about using the geometric method: first, make sure you draw right angles where right angles are needed, either by using a T-square (I use a little plastic one that cost me 59 cents), or by first lining up your points carefully; second, measure the dimensions of your original within the picture's margins only. Including the widths of the margins will always throw proportions off. (The exception would be if both they and the picture were squares, but in that case you have no problem of any kind in scaling.)

Cropping. This means marking only part of an original for reproduction. The illustrations available to you are only raw material. Take only what you want from each, cropping to emphasize what is relevant and excluding what is not. When reproducing a work of art, however, either include the entire picture (which is presumably designed to fill its space with some exactness) or identify the cropped version in your caption as a detail.

In deciding whether or where to crop, it is helpful to work with four sheets of white paper laid along the four sides, adjusting them until you have your new framing in sight within a true rectangle. Try to avoid including mysterious edges and fragments of figures, and keep in mind the proportions you want so that you can scale the cropped picture to fit your page.

Marking the illustration for cropping is best done with a grease (china marking) pencil at the margins, as shown here. The arrows point toward the new borders, in this case at all four sides. (Should you prefer no cropping at one edge, omit one pair of arrows.) If a grease pencil is used, the markings may be wiped off after the job is complete.

Occasionally you may want an irregular shape, even a cut-out silhouette. A simple irregular shape may be indicated by a paper mask laid over the original and fixed around the edges to prevent slipping. A cut-out or silhouette should be prepared with scissors and/or white paint by yourself or a skilled collaborator, using a print you can afford to mutilate for the purpose. If you mount the result on a white sheet, be careful not to use a paste or glue that will stain through or make even the smallest lump on the surface.

The most common way of ruining good pictures for reproduction is to write heavily on the back with a ball-point pen or sharp pencil. You should identify each illustration clearly, but if you cannot write gently on the back, then write on a separate slip of paper and tape it to the bottom edge.

Designing a Periodical

Virtually everything that makes good book design for the readers you are interested in also makes good design for the newsletter, magazine, or journal directed to the same group. In addition, there are two special considerations worth noting. The first stems from the fact that periodicals are really much larger enterprises than they appear to be when one sees only an individual issue. Because of this, small economies and small expenses can add up to quite large sums through repetition. That is the first consideration. Be conscious of the impact of multiplication over a year or two. The choice and use of paper, number of colors of inks, and type size are the main design concerns that need this kind of watching.

The second consideration has to do with the one-time ex-

Cropping a Picture

The Cropped Detail

pense. Some embellishments and niceties you might not allow yourself on a book might well be spent on a periodical if the benefits from the one outlay are visible over a long period and several thousand copies. A professional designer is an example. His fee for getting you started would not be large if it represented advice worth following over the next five years or more. Specially cast type and engravings for a masthead, seal, or identifying decorative illustrations, are other examples. Many of these economic aspects of design (and production) are made clear through the examples analyzed in the excellent slide-tape training kit "Newsletter Techniques," produced by the American Association for State and Local History.

Book Production

Your manuscript is ready, you know just what illustrations you want, and you have made all your design decisions with an eye to perfection and a willingness to become merely practical if necessary. Now it is time to hunt for the right printer. To find him, you will need your *specs*—your list of specifications, that is—in addition to the complete manuscript itself.

Specifications

At this stage you may wish to call your list "preliminary specifications," as a signal that you may be willing to modify details before contracting for the job. But the more detailed and clear you can be at this point, the more accurate a printer can be in quoting prices and terms that will stand. Below is a list of the items to be covered, with notes on each.

1. *Brief identifying description of the job.* This is just to give a name to the job, e.g., as "Book, *A History of Hamilton County.*"
2. *Length of text.* Count the number of lines in your typed text, with short lines counted as halves and omitting all subheads which have lines to themselves. Then find the length of an average line of your typewriting in characters

(letters *and spaces* both) by making an exact count of ten or so consecutive full lines and striking an average. Finally, multiply that figure (characters per line) by the number of lines, and enter the total as your character count for straight text.[1] (One standard basis for pricing typesetting is by the thousand characters.)

3. *Number of major parts or chapters which must start on a new page.*

4. *Number of subheadings which must be set on their own lines with extra space above them.* This and the count of separate parts (3, above) will help the printer see whether the job will require an unusual amount of paper or present special makeup problems.

5. *Footnote data.* The number of footnotes should be given, and also the number of lines; their placement should be indicated along with any change in type size. Thus: "Footnotes: 177 lines in 62 notes to be set at foot of pages in 8/10."

6. *Data on text for captions, running heads, index, and similar type separate from the main text.* On captions, summarize just as for footnotes. On index and running heads, estimate length requirements the best way you can. If you want an appendix or other special blocks of material not treated the same as the main text, this is the place to describe them.

7. *Data on illustrations and other graphic work.* Include the number and types of illustrations and other graphic work not to be set in type. Group by approximate sizes in terms of fractions of a page, e.g., "7 full-page halftones, 9 half-page halftones, and 4 full-page maps (line cuts)."

8. *Number of copies wanted.* Arriving at this figure is largely a marketing estimate, and the problem is discussed

1. I urged you earlier to type the entire manuscript in the same size of type with the same margins. If you did, fine, but if not, separate computations must be made at this point for each change of either kind. Suppose, for example, your first chapter was typed in pica type (10 characters per inch) and set at 70 spaces for width. If Chapter Two was done in elite (12 characters per inch) with margins at 90 (a ½-inch longer line), the difference is 30 percent, which will throw the whole calculation off.

below in that connection. You may want to ask the price for a conservative number of copies and also for another "price per additional 1,000" (which will be much lower), specifying that they be bound or unbound. Remember that the most expensive copy is the first.

9. *Binding requirements.* Binding needs should be described in the light of the discussion below on binding. You may wish to ask for alternative prices for two types, or make only general requirements. Thus "all Smyth-sewn and case-bound to library standards using [name your grade and brand] cloth, with silver stamped front and spine titles." Or "Wire saddle stiched with paper cover, printer to indicate cover stock used as basis for quotation."

Long as this list seems, it is not complete. Full specifications eventually must include the following items as well, although I am listing them separately here because at first you may prefer to ask the printer to take the initiative in suggesting these on the basis of his equipment:

10. *Page size* (trimmed)
11. *Paper stock for text* (and endleaves if used)
12. *Typefaces, including sizes, for text*
13. *Printing process to be used*

In addition, you may have a deadline date for delivery of the job which is crucial, and in that case you should indicate that you only want bids from those who feel they can meet it. It also means you should assure them that your manuscript will be ready by a certain date and that you can promise to take care of checking proofs and making the index within a specified time. Unless time is very short and important, it is better to wait until other matters are settled before asking the printer for a definite delivery date. The load on his work force and equipment will vary from week to week and season to season, and he cannot be expected to commit his time firmly to you until he knows you are ready to commit the job to him.

Choosing a Printer

If you are your own publisher, one of your main responsibilities will be to choose the right printer for the job at hand. There is no way this book can make the choice for you; it can only help point out some of the choices. And even the best advice will be useless if you are convinced that you know one great printer who can do everything the best and most economical way, or if you feel obligated by sentiment or social pressures to give the job to Uncle Charlie regardless. If you are free to make a choice, here are some suggestions for eliminating the worst prospects.

1. Avoid a printer who is too distant for frequent contact. There can be exceptions to this, and certainly it is not usually expected that you would need to visit the plant in person, but there is comfort in knowing that you can reach others at headquarters if the salesman is unable to meet all your needs. Many printing salesmen are not printers themselves and cannot offer the technical advice you may need on a complex job.

2. Avoid a printer whose shop is too large to give your job the individual attention it needs for best results. Once you gain some experience and know just what you want and how you want it done, you may be less cautious on this point, but the fact remains that big printers are at their best doing big jobs.

3. Avoid a printer whose shop is too small for your needs. Local historians will seldom have a job too large for any printer to handle in some fashion, but they may require a type of specialized work beyond the capabilities of some small shops.

4. Avoid any printer who seems reluctant. He should want your business, or something is already wrong with a relationship that needs to start strongly and optimistically if it is to weather the strains ahead. He may sense that he is unlikely to be able to meet your expectations but doesn't want to go into all the reasons. Or he may just be tired and crochety. You may never know the reason. But unless you have some personal

problem of your own in building business relations with people, there should be another printer down the road who will show that he wants to do your work.

One final note on timing: this can be of major importance in getting the best price and schedule. Printers have high fixed costs the year round, but many have slack seasons and will bid lower to keep their shops busy then. This is notably true of printers of school yearbooks.

A safe rule of thumb is to go to a printer who does a lot of publications similar to the one you have in mind. A good book printer may not be a good magazine printer.

To me the whole printing industry is a subject of endless interest, although I am not now and never have been any sort of printer myself. Good printing results from a kind of group marriage of art, science, technology, and business; nobody finishes learning about it if he is aiming for both excellence and efficiency. For those of you who share this interest, the books listed in the bibliography should be welcome teachers. All I can offer in the space of this book is an introduction to printing methods for those of you who, at least for the present, want only to get through the job at hand without major embarrassments. I will try to be quick and practical at the risk of being unscholarly and incomplete.

The three basic steps in printing are composition (including all proof stages), presswork, and binding, in that order.

Refining Specifications

In listing the items to be included in specifications for printing, those in the final group—page size, paper stock, type faces, and printing process—were treated separately as matters which might be settled after you had received bids on the basis of the rest of your needs (p. 128.) The reason for suggesting this delay in determining these four important questions is that once you have a low bidder, you also have a printer likely to have the most economical printing equipment for your job. Of course you should not commit yourself until you know the answers. But you should inquire at this point as to what he based his bid on and determine whether his choices are satisfactory to you in their promise of the quality you want.

For whatever type of press is offered by the low bidder, a certain range of papers is suitable and you can check on whether the stock offered provides the opacity, finish, and color you can accept. Negotiating a change should not be difficult, although the cost of paper is so large an item that any change must be expected to affect the bid price on the job. The printer will need to check also on the selection of sheet sizes available in the paper stock selected. He will consider not only the limitations of his press but also the efficiency with which any given sheet may be made up into pages. At this point he will also have to know whether his recommendation of a page size is acceptable to you. Minor changes are usually negotiable here, but any significant increase in page size would inevitably raise the cost unless there were offsetting economies in page format such as the adoption of double columns. If you plan for a single column of type, however, you will normally use between 4 and 4½ inches width for the type itself, so total page widths of between 5½ and 6 inches will allow ample margins. A page wider than 6 inches is an expensive luxury unless justified by something other than white space. Page depth may be adjusted within the maximum set by the decision on the page width. Your printer will calculate the maximum, and from that you may cut short if you wish but, just as in cutting cloth, you can't cut long.

Finally, look at your printer's specimen type faces, starting with the one he had in mind in making his bid. Negotiations are possible here within the limits of the choices he has in stock. Major changes in size or spacing may also affect the total paper required. Now is also the time to agree on display types and any special needs for the cover design. If there is a special titling face you want and cannot find among the printer's specimens, inquire about it anyway. He may be able to buy a few lines of it locally.

In advising that the final typographic choices be postponed

until so late, I do not mean to minimize their importance. Certainly if you cannot feel comfortable with the type your low bidder can offer for the text it is time to look seriously at your second lowest bidder. Printers are naturally partial toward their own stock, and they can be very loose in what they consider equivalent to any type you name. You have to trust your own eye. To my eye, for example, Press Roman is not at all a substitute for Times Roman, but Caledonia is, although it is fatter, and Baskerville would be acceptable if there were space to set it one point larger.

Composition

   Composition is the preparation of type and illustrations for the press. The specialist in this work is called a compositor. Any sort of work may be composed in some fashion by one of three methods—*hot metal, photocomposition,* or *direct image.* These last two are sometimes referred to as *cold type.*
   1. *Hot Metal Type.* This is the traditional raised lettering cast in single lines (called *slugs*) or assembled one letter at a time by hand. It is typesetting as Gutenberg invented it over five hundred years ago, except that he used wooden types. Today, hand-set type is too laborious and expensive except for titles and similarly short operations. Linecasting machines produce the bulk of metal type, and are especially adapted to jobs that require adjustments in spacing and corrections of errors right up to the last minute. It is partly for this reason that daily newspapers are mostly still dependent on cast metal type. Linotype, Intertype, and Monotype are the manufacturers of the equipment for hot type as well as the source of many of the type faces used. Most American shops use one of the first two brands, which are interchangeable. Hot metal typesetting can be used for letterpress or offset printing.
   Metal engravings and their plastic equivalents sometimes used for short press runs are known as *cuts,* and are used only when the job is printed by letterpress. They are made up in the pages with the metal type. A *line cut* shows only black and white solid areas—no grays. It is suitable for simple drawings,

Printing Methods

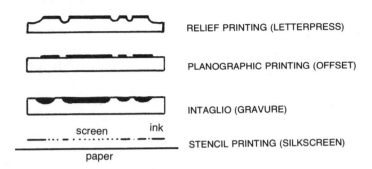

diagrams and some maps. A *halftone cut* translates the original (a photograph, for example) into a pattern of tiny black dots of varying sizes and spacings so that the eye sees them as shades of gray. The translation from solids to dots is accomplished by photographing the original through a fine screen. The finer the screen the more accurate the reproduction and the greater the need for a smooth paper for printing it. This is why halftone cuts originally made for newspaper use (about 85 lines-per-inch screen) look so coarse and gray when reprinted in books on smoother paper. Conversely, when a cut made on a fine screen—say over 110 lines per inch—is printed by letterpress on rough, absorbent paper, it looks blotchy and too contrasty. Note also that halftone engravings cannot be made satisfactorily from images that have already been screened except with great care and added expense. It is safest to work from a photographic print even if it is a copy made from a screened halftone.

2. *Photocomposition.* In this process, the operator types on the keyboard of a machine which programs a punch-tape or magnetic tape which in turn directs the photographing of one letter at a time on a master film or paper print. Changes in letter sizes and faces can be accommodated, usually without interruptions. Speed is limited mostly by the keyboard operation and, of course, by any corrections required. The width of a line of type may be extended beyond the limit for line cast-

ing machines, which is 30 picas, or about 5 inches. Display type may be produced on a separate and simpler machine. Both display and text typefaces are available in a wide range of styles.

Illustrations to be used in photocomposition are handled the same way by the customer as those for metal composition and look the same in the final result. But they are less expensive because their preparation is entirely with cameras, screens, and film. No etching of letterpress metal plates is involved. As noted earlier, there is also greater flexibility in the location of illustrations on the page when photocomposition is used.

3. *Direct Image Composition (strike-on)*. This and the next method (stencil) are the least expensive forms of composition, especially if you are willing to do the typing yourself. With this method, you may deliver from the hands of an ordinary typist pages of camera-ready copy which will look exactly like your final printed pages, illustrations and all, except for any reduction in the page size (and therefore the print size) you may wish to specify. It is also possible to have only the sizes of the illustrations reduced by the printer before he fits them in the blank areas you have allotted to them on the typed pages.

To make a success of this technique, you need a good typist, an electric typewriter with a carbon ribbon, and a willingness to give careful attention to details of margins, page makeup, and neatness in correcting errors. Any electric typewriter in good working order will give a more even impression than a manual, and the carbon ribbon, while not essential, is preferred as yielding a more photogenic result.

Of the electric typewriters to be found in office use, the IBM Selectric has the advantage of allowing some changes in typefaces. For any given machine the choices are limited, but they always include italics. Changing over requires a pause to unsnap and replace the rotating ball which carries the type font. If you adopt this machine for your work, do not count on using the extra tall letters (Orator type) for good reproduction, since the tops of these letters are often struck too lightly against the platen to give a sufficiently uniform black imprint. In preparing camera-ready copy, it is convenient to use paper preprinted with margins in light blue. Light blue will not photograph, so all proof corrections should also be made with a blue pencil lightly handled.

If it bothers you that your product will end up looking like what it is—typewriting rather than conventional "print"—there are three things you might do. The first two involve the use of one of the specially designed typewriters. The third is to be persuaded that you really should not be bothered about it.

The special typewriters require some explanation. Ordinary typewriting has two characteristics that distinguish it from other printing. One is that each letter is given the same space on the line as every other. The second is that spaces between both letters and words are preset so that the lines are of uneven length along the right-hand margin of the page. That is, the lines cannot be "justified" so that they will all stretch the same length and fit within straight margins at both sides, as lines of newspaper and book columns do. But if you are willing to pay more, there are typewriters that offer proportional spacing of letters (the IBM *Executive,* the Underwood *Raphael,* and the Hermes *Ambassador* among them), or machines equipped to justify lines, such as the VariTyper,

Proportional Spacing

This is the difference proportional spacing makes.
This is the difference proportional spacing makes.

Reproduced above is a line of type with conventional and proportional spacing. The top line is from an IBM Composer typewriter using 11-point Press Roman, one of the more highly condensed faces in common use. The bottom line is from a Remington elite typewriter. All conventional typewriters give equal space to each character, whether i or w.

made by Addressograph-Multigraph, or the IBM Composer. The latter is the simpler and more economical to operate of the two. It is widely used for the preparation of publications and may be rented as well as purchased. A variety of type styles are available and easily interchanged.

Even without expensive equipment, incidentally, it is quite possible to get an even right-hand margin if you are willing to take the trouble. You only need to go through a second typing, planning your lines so they come out even. This can give a presentable result if your machine has half-spaces and you are typing fairly long lines. But if you have neither (which is usually the case when this practice is adopted, as for double-column newsletters) the result makes for jerky reading to the point of distraction.

In my own view, the practical advantages of typewriter composition are lost as soon as the requirement of a neat (justified) right-hand margin enters in, and the best solution for the typist is not to let it in. If you are going to work from typewriting, print your pages ragged right.

If you choose this route and meet with some complaints, here are some points in rebuttal. First, readability is improved with adoption of a ragged right margin, since spacing between words is uniform and the number of divided words at the ends of lines is minimized. Second, it is only custom that supports the preference for straight margins on both sides. There is nothing aesthetically absolute or profound about it. (Does a poet ask to have his lines of verse evened at the ends?) Finally, it should be noted that several book designers of the highest reputation have advocated giving up the rigidly justified line. Christopher Lehman-Haupt had his distinguished history of *Bookmaking in America* set with a ragged right margin justified only to avoid hyphens and excessively short lines. Marshall Lee approves the practice and offers a sample of it on page 50 of his *Bookmaking*. The rest of his book was set in justified lines, he apologized, because the machinery "favored" it.

Typing the text of your publication as camera-ready copy does not commit you to typing the title page and chapter headings as well. For display type there are also direct image techniques. Sheets of black stick-on or rub-on letters are sold under various brand names, and an experienced hand can get excellent results with them. There are also labeling machines which print on a transparent tape which is then cut and fitted on the page. Any printing shop with cold type equipment will have such devices and should be willing to produce titles and headings from them for the customer who is having his text set on a typewriter at home.

Stencil Composition. A second form of direct image composition is the stencil method. The office duplicator has long been a familiar tool in schools as well as offices, and recent technology has added to its versatility. The basic process is simple. You cut through a sheet of plastic with your typewriter keys, a stylus, or an engraving tool, to let ink pass through from the front to create an image on paper pressed behind it.[2] Paper and page size requirements are fairly strict (with letter- or legal-size Mimeo Bond being the normal stock), and the press run is limited by the endurance of the stencil to 1,000 copies or a little more. The quality of printing is at best equal to that of a manual typewriter in appearance. But it is by far the cheapest printing within these limits on producing the text, especially if you type the stencils at home. Thanks to the recent development of an electromagnetic stencil-cutting device, complemented by simpler patterns and templates for the stylus, the Gestetner Company now offers users of the process a chance to reproduce a variety of large types for headings and gray tones even from photographs. One need not buy the electromagnetic extras; a dealer can handle occasional needs with a small charge per stencil. For economy in small editions of black-and-white printing, the stencil process is the first one to consider. The manufacturers are Gestetner and

---

2. This does not describe the "ditto" machine or hectograph, which is a planographic rather than stencil process, and is omitted from consideration here because of its short press-run capacity and its inability to print with black ink. It is useful, of course, for classroom materials, office circulars, and menus.

Addressograph Multigraph. Mimeograph is a trade name
owned by the latter firm.

Proofreading

Once the type has been set, the composition stage would be
complete and your publication would be ready for the press if
neither you nor the compositor were human. Understanding
their own capacity for error, printers routinely submit several
(usually three) proof copies of the text for the customer's review. Proofs are printed on a special press, or, in the case of
cold type they may be Xeroxed, so they do not show exactly
what the final presswork will accomplish. But a proof should
be treated as if it represented the finished job. Type that is
blurred, misaligned, or unevenly inked should be called to the
printer's attention in order to make sure that he takes responsibility for judging which faults need correction and which are
merely incidental to the proof sheets.

As the customer, you are expected to return one set of
proofs marked "approved as corrected" with your dated signature and the original manuscript (without changes), plus a
dummy of the page layout made from another set of proofs,
plus any new text or illustrations not supplied earlier. Something will be said below about each item in this package. First,
however, a note of caution about expenses.

All the changes you call for as corrections of printer's errors at whatever stage they first appear are made at no charge
to the customer. But any correction of an error in the original
copy given the printer and any change that results from the
author or editor changing his mind, will be charged for at a
rate above that for the original typesetting. Obviously, it pays
to submit clean copy the first time and then not change your
mind. Errors of fact, of course, should be corrected at any
expense at any time before going to press.

Although proofreading requires the participation of several individuals, one of them must take charge. The chief
proofreader need not be the author or editor, but it must be
someone willing and able to see that the total job is accomp-

lished and the results communicated to the printer. The questions that will be answered when the proofs are approved are these: (1) Does the printing follow the copy as submitted? (2) Does the text still make sense? (3) Are there technical errors (regardless of whose fault) in spelling, capitalization, punctuation, spacing, or alignment? Because the range of questions is so broad, it is important to reread proofs several times with a different focus each time. You cannot, for example, read for sense and for spacing at the same time.

In every reading, standard proofreader's marks should be used. A display of the full list has not been included here because it should be available elsewhere on your bookshelf—in the University of Chicago Press *Manual of Style, Webster's Collegiate Dictionary*, and many other references. Remember that the printer will look only in the margins of the proofs for your corrections and queries. If you have a problem in deciding how to mark something clearly, write it out in the margin so that it is clear to you, and then tag that page to remind you to speak to the printer's representative about it when you return the proofs. Get in the habit of circling all such queries and notes, however, to protect you against the possiblity that they may be set in type as inserts.

The answer to the first question—"Does it follow the copy?"—requires a word-by-word comparison with the copy itself. Some surprising (but entirely human) errors will show up in no other way. Thus if the sentence "Worthington returned on December 17" were printed as "Washington returned on December 7," the plausibility of the reading would conceal its corruption of the text from anyone not alert to the original message. Many publishers insist on having the proof read silently by one person while another reads the original copy aloud, punctuation marks and all. This is the safest method, although like any other, it requires undistracted attention. However this reading is arranged, its primary purpose is to discover printer's errors. When they are found, it is a good idea to mark them with a distinctively colored pencil. (Be sure, however, that such departures *are* errors, and not favors from a typesetter who spells or spaces better than you did.)

One set of proofs is normally sent to the author for his review and return. It is hard to know just what an author will focus on as he reads. Most probably it will be the sense of the text. Whatever corrections he comes up with, they may require translation into standard marks. And they may require some consultation and negotiation if he seems to have been excessively changeable. (If you are the author, of course none of this will present a problem.)

Assuming that someone has read the proof once for the sense of it, a final reading (or two) is still in order. This time attention should be focused on details that could not be scrutinized when attention was being given to the first two questions. Use the latest edition of a desk dictionary to check on hyphens, word division at the ends of lines, and similar details. Watch for inconsistencies in the style adopted for capitalization, dates, commas, and use of numerals. Scan the lines and margins for alignments and indentions. Certain combinations of letters will create an optical illusion of unevenness, and a ruler is called for. Ask for corrections only when you find actual irregularities that you expect the reader to notice.

Making a Dummy

When proofreading is far enough along so that any changes affecting the number of lines of text have been caught, one set of proofs can be dedicated to the preparation of a *dummy*, or *paste-up*. This is actually a step in the design process rather than a part of proofreading, but it is a step that should be taken now in order to give the printer a guide to the next proof stage, which is the one showing how each page is made up. Cut up one set of proofs (they need not show minor corrections), and paste in place on sheets of page-size paper the blocks of type you want to appear on each page, leaving measured spaces for illustrations, captions, chapter headings and other breaks. Mark each page with its number. The page number which is to be printed—called the *folio*—should also be located where you want it (outside margins of pages, center top, bottom center?) and directions on this and similar matters of spacing should be written out on the dummy.

A second set of page numbers is also welcomed by printers. This set starts with the first page of type (half title or title page) and continues consecutively throughout, with blank pages included (marked, for example, "page 4 blank") and all the numbers in this series circled to distinguish them. This series of circled numbers is not only a convenience to the printer in case he spills the whole collection on the floor; it is also important to you as the customer because it tells you the total number of pages that will run through the press. For example, if you are budgeting a 128-page book, your count must begin with the first page in this series and end with the last. The reader who sees only the numbered pages in print (the folios) may call it a 120-page book. He does not count the unnumbered title page, copyright page, foreword, table of contents, blank pages, and others which are not given printed numbers. But you must see them because you must pay for the paper and the presswork.

Once you (and here "you" means the chief proofreader and dummy-maker) have assembled and submitted the corrected first proofs and dummy, the printer will return a second set of proofs. These are *page proofs*. At this point, your responsibility is to read again, watching now especially for (1) corrections made as directed (by checking against the first proofs, which should also have been returned for this purpose), (2) new errors made while these corrections were being set—e.g., "Wortington relearned on Dezember 17", (3) spaces and margins again, since whole blocks of type have been moved since you last saw them, and (4) errors in the setting of any new copy submitted with the first proofs. The latter usually includes picture captions, page numbers, and a variety of other additions. Look again also at the title page and chapter heads. But remember that author's changes at this stage will be more expensive than before. Try to hold them to within the page spaces already given.

If an index is to be prepared, this is the time to start on it, and a separate set of page proofs will be needed for the purpose. The technique of preparing an index is discussed in several books cited in the bibliography. When the job is done and submitted, however, remember that it is new copy subject to careful proofreading apart from the rest of the material. It also needs to be pasted up on dummy pages within the space planned for it.

If you are printing by photo-offset, still a third proof stage may be obtained should you wish to arrange for it. This is the *blue line* or *vandyke*. It is a blueprint of the corrected page proofs with illustrations in place and pages trimmed, all folded and assembled as a facsimile of the final publication in every respect but color, paper stock, and binding. This proof is important when illustrations are used, as it is your only chance to see how they are cropped, reproduced, and placed. Page trimming and all alignments may also be checked now. For letterpress work no blueprint is made, but the inking of final page proofs should be given a critical look again for evenness.

Proofreading may be a dull chore at times, but the cost of neglecting it is high. Those embarrassing errors in the final result are as permanent as the rest of the publication.

Presswork

Not every form of type composition is compatible with every kind of press. Type set in hot metal is adaptable to all presses, either directly as relief printing on a letterpress or indirectly through the use of reproduction proofs *(repros)* from which offset plates are made. All other forms of composition are suitable only for offset presses. (Gravure is also an option technically, but it is economical only when used for long runs of illustrated publications.) The simpler offset presses, such as Multilith, will handle most forms of composition including color and good (though not excellent) reproduction of halftone illustrations. Stencil composition is prepared for an office duplicating machine and to use it any other way would be uneconomical. Should a stencil-printed publication remain in demand after the first printing is exhausted, however, a second printing might be on a small offset machine such as Multilith rather than returning to worn stencils or re-cutting them. The change would only involve cutting up one good copy of the original printing for offset masters or plates to be made from the pages.

Having planned in consultation with your printer to make an outstanding printing result possible, you come eventually to the point where you must stand aside and hope for the best. Even small presses do their work with great rapidity. Quality control while the wheels are spinning is the responsibility of expert operators, and customers or other anxious amateurs are not welcomed near the machinery. The exceptional case would be a four–color printing job when the customer's approval of final adjustments in the inking may be wanted. But as a rule, press operators work alone. Their customers can only see samples of past results and hope for equally good performance on their own job.

Binding–the Practicalities

Binding has been discussed as an element in the book's design, but its engineering and economic aspects are equally important. One choice of binding might well represent half of the book's production costs and still be the best choice for the treatment of that book. It depends on what is to be bound and how much there is of it. Starting with the least expensive and taking them in order up the cost scale, the varieties of binding are as follows.

Wire stitching, the least expensive binding, divides into *side wire* stitching and *saddle wire* stitching. In both, the wires are simply staples. If you have up to around 30 unfolded sheets (leaves) and a paper cover, side wire stitching could be a reasonable choice. The staples grip along the inside margins from cover to cover. (See illustration in Figure 5). After the staples are in, a strip of tape may be wrapped around the spine covering the staples and ends of the leaves. Printing on such a spine is impractical, however. Side wire stitching makes for a tight, compact booklet that will not bulge or spring open. On the contrary, it wants to spring shut whenever you let go of it, and this is its main drawback. If you choose this binding, allow generous inside page margins because the staples will be cutting into them. And keep a bookmark handy.

Saddle wire stitching is favored for many booklets of up to about 64 pages (more if the paper is low in bulk), but they must come to the stitching machine in one gathering of folded pages. The staples are punched through the back at the fold as the collated pages ride on a moving saddle from the folding machine. Because of their placement, the staples need only grip 18 sheets to bind 64 pages. The maximum number of pages is thus not limited by staple strength, but rather by the limited number of sheets which can be folded in one gathering. Somewhere around 64 pages the paper's resistance to folding becomes noticeable in an excessive springiness. Even after being subjected to long pressure, the booklet may tend to open itself to its middle page, and when closed assume a somewhat oval shape when seen from the top.

Perfect binding is the modest name given to a method that is in fact very good for certain purposes. Books larger than those adapted to wire stitching, if designed for soft covers and not required to last indefinitely, may be very securely bound by simply trimming, roughing, and gluing together the back edges of the pages. A strip of gauze may be stretched over the back edge afterward, but it is the glue which does the work as it penetrates a short way between the pages. The cover is likewise glued on at the spine. Modern adhesives are stronger than paper while they last—test your telephone book's binding for an example—but to depend on their strength for longer than five years of regular use is probably unwise.

Smyth-sewn binding is the traditional method used for hard-cover books. It is permanent and capable of holding together the largest volumes. Each gathering (signature) of pages is secured to the others by threads looped and crossed and then secured under a gauze strip backing glued on. Even if each signature is of 32 pages, the thread has to pass through

Five Types of Book Binding

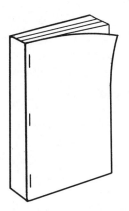

1. SIDE WIRE STITCHING

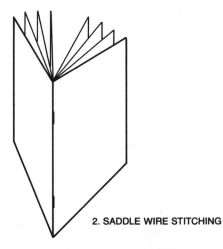

2. SADDLE WIRE STITCHING

Glue applied after folds
have been removed

paper cover

plastic comb

3. MECHANICAL BINDING

4. PERFECT BINDING

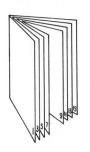

A sixteen-page
signature

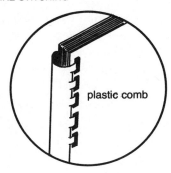

Folded and gathered sheets
(made up of six signatures)

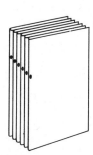

Smyth-
sewn

glue on
spine

endpapers

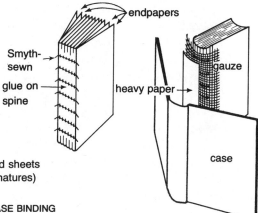

heavy paper

gauze

case

5. CASE BINDING

only eight sheets, so the strain is well distributed. The pages are tightly held and yet the book will lie open. Hard covers (case bindings) are attached by extending the gauze backing under the heavy endpapers and gluing, although in the best traditional bindings heavy cords or tapes are also glued across the spine and into the cover under the end papers. This accounts for the origin of the ribbing on the spines of many older books, although ribs are also sometimes merely decorative stamping of the cover cloth.

Mechanical binding is the spiral notebook wire or (more commonly now) plastic series of loops which grip through precut holes in the paper and cover. The pages lie perfectly flat when open, though they do not come flush together in the center (the *gutter*). Some types also permit new pages to be inserted in place, though without the same ease as a loose-leaf ring binder permits. The appearance is always somewhat informal, the spine bulging wider than the cover, and the plastic spine, which is rounded, does not easily accept printing. There is no protection of the paper from dust or moisture at the spine. With age, wire rusts and plastic becomes brittle. Workbooks, datebooks, and calendars are typical choices for mechanical binders because of the importance of having the pages lie flat or hang straight.

Packaging for Shipping

If most copies of your book are to be shipped individually through the mails, the cost per delivered copy will be affected by two considerations: the postal rates bear most heavily on the first pound, and a safe container for a single book is a relatively expensive item. Only the large publishers can have cardboard packing tailored to fit each book. One versatile packing on the market now is the padded bag which you fill from one end and staple shut. Less expensive is a flexible corrugated paper which can be used as a wrapper (sealing the ends and taping lengthwise) or to sandwich the book. A slim paperback booklet, of course, may safely be entrusted to a sturdy kraft paper envelope.

Promoting and Marketing Your Book

Your book should be promoted and sold properly, but you should not have to take primary responsibility for these tasks, especially if you have already nursed the book along from conception through research, writing, editing, design, and production. For one thing, you are going to be too tired, and very possibly tired of seeing and thinking about it. Fresh energy is needed, and different talents are demanded. An organizational connection is almost essential if the product is not to remain indefinitely in stacks of cartons from the printer. Each of the brief suggestions below assumes that you have some help at this stage.

Ideally, you know at press time where a large number of your new book is going and already have the money pocketed. You have presold the book. You may have obligated a certain number of copies to an organization in return for a subsidy. Or you may have sold subscriptions in advance. Subscriptions are a routine procedure for periodicals, but in the case of books the prospective customer must be persuaded to send his money (or at least his order) in advance of the actual publication date. This means he cannot see a copy or read a review. To compensate him, you might offer a prepublication discount and a 10-day free return privilege. But do not waste money by offering such inducements to a group of prospects who will probably be just as likely to buy at the full price. If most of your market is among institutions and individuals who will either want the book badly or not at all, you might as well wait and announce the same price to everyone.

Once the book is off the press, there is again the possibility of moving it in quantities by seeking out one purchaser willing to pay one bill for a group. For example, can you find one buyer on behalf of all the public and school libraries? Or do you have a booklet which might be used as a gift (not *your* gift) to newly arrived families through the Welcome Wagon hostess or her equivalent? Sample copies of a periodical can be promoted the same way at the outset.

Bookstores, giftshops, and even drugstores might be asked

to take consignments. Decide what commission you can afford to offer and treat them all alike, though some may be ready to handle your book free as a gesture of support to the sponsoring organization. In any case, do not offer anyone commissions or discounts so large that they cut into your actual production expenses. The time for that may come later, but it should not even be considered within the first two years of the life of a book intended to have some lasting value.

Selling one copy at a time is simple once you get the orders coming in—which brings us to the subject of advertising. As applied to a publication in local history, the subject is not unmanageably large, because there are probably only X number of people out there who would buy the book whether they have heard of it once or a hundred times. Your job is simply to broadcast, not to browbeat. And you have two basic ways of doing it: (1) through the appropriate publications and other media, and (2) by direct mail advertisement.

Mass media (to use the most inclusive term) should be used for publicity, but through paid advertisements only as a last resort. More effective are the news features in the press and reviews wherever you can get them. Review copies with an inserted note giving the publication date and price may be sent to the book review editor of any publication you feel may publish a review—but be sure it has published reviews before. Interviews with the author, if invited, should be accepted, book in hand. If you get an interview on a network television talk show, stop reading this now and start arranging for a second printing.

Direct mail campaigns can be extremely effective for selling local and regional history. The same principles apply whether the mailing is in advance of publication or following it. You need good mailing lists, a good flyer, and a budget.

The flyer, or whatever form the announcement takes, should be designed with the special groups it is directed to clearly in mind. If one kind of message or appeal does not seem to fit them all, perhaps a duplicated letter could be substituted or added for a particular group. But for economy and most uses, an 8½-by 11-inch sheet of good colored paper stock may be printed on one side, folded twice, stapled and then addressed on the outside as a self-mailer. The sales message should be checked for accuracy and tone with the author. If you are the author, let someone else edit. An order form may be printed across the bottom for the reader to clip. You may receive a few more orders if you enclose a self-addressed and postage-paid reply card, but in most cases not enough to justify the added expense to yourself. As to your own postage, First Class adds up in cost so rapidly that if you are working through an organization that has a bulk mailing permit you should almost certainly use it.

Address lists may be obtained in several ways. Firms specializing in direct mail selling usually offer to take your material and send it to everyone in a given category for a lump sum. If you are trying to reach a special group scattered across the country and hard to locate, such services may be worth investigating. But local and statewide lists of the kind you probably need most are usually available free in various published directories. Librarians are good at finding these, and several units of state government can be counted on to issue such lists periodically. Local historical societies are covered by the AASLH Directory, and museums by the American Association of Museums Directory. If the subscribers to a special interest periodical seem likely prospects (and not already covered on other lists), query the publisher as to terms for his list. He may charge less for services similar to those of a commercial firm, and in any case he will have the most up-to-date list because it is the one he depends on himself.

A Note on Pricing

The exact sales price of a publication should not be announced until all possible cost figures are in and a decision cannot be delayed. Of course you should set goals early and figure an approximate price. But the facts you need for a final decision on a new publication cannot be known or in some cases even closely estimated until late in the process. The facts you need include the actual costs of printing and binding, editorial and design services, royalties and permissions, advertising (don't forget the postage bill), packaging, shipping, and free copies. Then you will know your break-even price if every copy is sold. What margin you want to provide for discounts to retailers, spoilage, mailing casualties, uncollected bills, and buyer resistance is up to you. Suppose you have a thousand books actually for sale, and calculate that it will have cost you six dollars for each copy delivered. Especially if you are selling one copy at a time, it is unrealistic to expect to collect on every one without a mishap, so six dollars is too low even as a break-even estimate. Indeed, unless your retail price is set at ten dollars, your sales to bookstores at their customary 40 percent discount will only enable you to break even on those actually sold through them. Some publishers plan on taking a slight loss on bookstore sales, expecting to make up the difference through direct mail orders. Nevertheless, most retail prices are set at three to four times the actual manufacturing costs. In the final analysis there is no correct formula to cover all cases entirely. The terms on which any services were donated or subsidies given must be respected so that the distribution of income does not create misunderstandings or antagonisms. To put it another way, those who gave out of love should know how their love will be requited.

Fortunately for this world, those who write local history are usually content with the self-rewarding love of seeing a job well done. I have assumed that to be your motive at the start, and hope the assumption remains good at the end. At the same time, I wish you many new editions.

Bibliography

Introductory and General

Titles selected for inclusion in the three sections that follow this one have been rigorously limited to those the author feels are the most useful at the present time from among the many which deal with the various special topics. Availability has also been a consideration. Wherever possible, titles have been chosen which may be obtained in a library of medium size or through the mail. Additional titles may be found in the bibliographies listed and in references contained in many of the books recommended as starting points on their specialties.

The only other book of the same scope as the present work is Donald Dean Parker, *Local History: How to Gather It, Write, It, and Publish It* (New York: Social Research Council, 1944). Republished and long kept in print, the book met a real demand, but the times have changed and the book has not. I have tried to study the virtues of Parkers' book while making a fresh start in writing this one.

On the research and writing of history—but not publishing it —several excellent books directed to American college and graduate students have appeared in recent years. They are nearly all worth some attention, but I would single out Barzun and Graff's *The Modern Researcher* as the strongest, and also recommend Cantor and Schneider's *How to Study History*. Both are cited more fully below, and both are broader in scope than their titles imply, although neither deals directly with the special problems of local history.

For the local historian who wants to freshen his understanding of the broader themes of national history, my first recommendation is John A. Garraty's *The American Nation*, 4th ed. (New York: Harper & Row and American Heritage, 1979) or the author's later abridgement, *A Short History of the American Nation* (1974). Another fine survey is

John M. Blum, et al., *The National Experience*, 4th ed. (New York: Harcourt Brace Jovanovich, n.d.) It is no secret that these were written as college texts, but you might be surprised at how readable they are.

Before beginning the main bibliographical listing, I want to mention the Technical Leaflet series published by the American Association for State and Local History. These pamphlets are bound into the Association's monthly magazine *History News* and are also available separately by mail. I would recommend the following as especially pertinent, pithy, and authoritative:

On Research:

Creigh, Dorothy Weyer. "Ethnic Groups, Part One: Research for the Local Society." Technical Leaflet No. 108. In *History News* 33 (September 1978).

Ellsworth, Linda. "The History of a House: How to Trace It." Technical Leaflet No. 89. In *History News* 24 (September 1976).

Hale, Richard W., Jr. "Methods of Research for the Amateur Historian." Technical Leaflet No. 21. In *History News* 24 (September 1969).

Miller, Carolynne L. "Genealogical Research: A Basic Guide." Technical Leaflet No. 14. In *History News* 24 (March 1969).

Newman, John J. "Cemetery Transcribing: Preparations and Procedures." Technical Leaflet No. 9. In *History News* 26 (May 1971).

Sahli, Nancy. "Local History Manuscripts: Sources, Uses, and Preservation." Technical Leaflet No. 115. In *History News* 34 (May 1979).

Warner, Sam B., Jr. "Writing Local History: The Use of Social Statistics." Rev. ed. Technical Leaflet No. 7. In *History News* 25 (October 1970).

On Publications

Alderson, William T., editor. "Marking and Correcting Copy for Your Printer." Technical Leaflet No. 51. In *History News* 24 (June 1969).

Derby, Charlotte S. "Reaching Your Public: The Historical Society Newsletter." Technical Leaflet No. 39. In *History News* 22 (January 1967).

Gore, Gary G. "Phototypesetting: Getting the Most for Your Money." Technical Leaflet No. 103. In *History News* 33 (January 1978).

Walket, John J., Jr. "Publishing in the Historical Society." Technical Leaflet No. 34. In *History News* 21 (April 1966).

Most book titles listed below are not stocked by dealers, and a few are out of print. If library copies are unavailable or unsatisfactory, books may be ordered from some publishers through dealers or in the used book market through specialists in that trade. The latest *Books in Print* should first be consulted in a library. Addresses of publishers may also be found there at the end of volume II.

Researching

Adams, James Truslow. *Atlas of American History.* New York: Charles Scribner's Sons, 1943. A companion to his *Dictionary of American History,* this atlas also contains 147 specially drawn maps in chronological order and a useful index. See also Paullin's atlas, below, which has a different emphasis.

America: History and Life: Part A: Article Abstracts. Clio Press, American Bibliographical Center. A periodical first issued in 1964, this is now part of a set, of which Part B is the *Index to Book Reviews* and Part C *American History Bibliography.* The part with the abstracts covers about 600 periodicals, with titles pertaining to each state grouped together. Most college and major public libraries subscribe.

American Association for State and Local History. *Directory of Historical Societies and Agencies in the United States and Canada.* 11th ed., Nashville: AASLH, 1978. Basic data, including telephone numbers, on nearly 5,000 organizations arranged by state and province. One of the indexes is of societies by special interest.

American Historical Association. *Writings on American History.* 35 vols., covering 1902-1961 except for 1941-1947; various publishers and compilers. There is one cumulative index covering 1902-1940; other volumes are individually indexed. Local and regional titles of both books and articles are well represented in this thorough and important reference tool. Its successor since 1975 has been covering articles only but appears with less delay: *Writings on American History: A Subject Bibliography of Articles.* Millwood, N.Y.: Kraus International. Look for these in the larger libraries.

American Library Directory: A Classified List of Libraries in the United States and Canada with Personnel and Statistical Data. New York: R. R. Bowker (biennial). Geographical by state, then city, giving all the essential data for contacts plus notes on any special collections. It covers over 24,000 U.S. and 2,000 Canadian libraries.

Ash, Lee, ed. *Subject Collections: A Guide to Special Book Collections in Libraries.* 5th ed., New York: R. R. Bowker, 1978. Over 1,200 pages, with a good index.

Baum, Willa K. *Oral History and the Local Historical Society.* 2nd ed., Nash
    ville: The American Association for State and Local History, 1971. A fine
    handbook of 62 pages, with illustrations and a bibliography. This is a
    revised second edition of a booklet originally published by the Conference
    of California Historical Societies, Stockton.
Benjamin, Mary. *Autographs: A Key to Collecting.* New York: Walter R.
    Benjamin Autographs, rev. ed., 1963. Written by a dealer for collectors,
    but useful for the researcher as detective. Not much has been written in this
    field, but this is well written. Out of print.
Blumenson, John J.-G. *Identifying American Architecture: A Pictorial Guide to
    Styles and Terms, 1600-1945.* Rev. ed. Nashville: American Association for
    State and Local History, 1981. A compact book with more than 200 il-
    lustrations covering 39 styles and many details, neatly organized. Available
    in hard cover from co-publisher W. W. Norton & Co., Inc., 500 Fifth
    Avenue, New York, N.Y. 10110; available in paperback from the American
    Association for State and Local History, 1400 Eighth Avenue, South,
    Nashville, Tenn. 37203. See also Whiffen, below.
Brigham, Clarence S. *History and Bibliograhy of American Newspapers,
    1690-1820.* 2 vols., Worcester, Mass.: American Antiquarian Society, 1947.
    Supplement, 1976, Greenwood Press. Alphabetical by city within each
    state; notes on publishers, printers, and depository locations. Indexes. See
    also Gregory, below.
Brooks, Philip C. *Research in Archives: The Use of Unpublished Primary
    Sources.* Chicago: University of Chicago Press, 1969. A short book, but
    broad in the scope of good advice from a veteran of 30 years with the
    National Archives who was then Director of the Harry S. Truman Library.
Brown, Lloyd A. *The Story of Maps.* Boston: Little, Brown, 1949. Beginning
    with antiquity and covering the globe. Brown says little about American
    cartographers or maps but provides a reference on basic questions of
    methods and apparatus, and an excellent bibliography of works issued prior
    to 1949.
Child, Sargent B., and D. P. Holmes. *Checklist of Historical Records Survey
    Publications.* Work Projects Administration Technical Series, Research and
    Records Bibliography No. 7. Washington, 1943. Reprinted in 1969 by the
    Genealogical Publishing Co., Baltimore.
Clark, Thomas D. *The Southern Country Editor.* Indianapolis: Bobbs-Merrill,
    1948; reprinted Gloucester, Mass.: Peter Smith, 1964. Deserving attention
    from students of other regions where the small town newspaper has not
    been as thoroughly studied. Covers the years 1865-1917.
Condit, Carl W. *American Building: Materials and Techniques from the First
    Colonial Settlements to the Present.* Chicago: University of Chicago Press,
    1973, paperback. Condit writes lucidly of the engineering of construction
    rather than of styles of design. He has also written separate volumes on
    nineteenth- and twentieth-century building.

Doane, Gilbert S. *Searching for Your Ancestors: The How and Why of Genealogy.* 5th ed., New York: Bantam Books, 1980 (paper). Originally published in 1930, it remains the standard.

Evans, Hilary; Mary Evans; and Andra Nelki. *The Picture Researcher's Handbook: An International Guide to Picture Sources—and How to Use Them.* New York: Charles Scribner's Sons, 1974. The introductory text is good on how to identify various techniques (though Ivins, below, is more thorough on prints), on costs of reproduction services, and on credits. The guide describes twelve U.S. and Canadian public collections, nine "commercial historical" collections (e.g., Culver, Bettmann), and sixteen "commercial modern" sources. Indexed. See also Frankenberg, below.

Fischer, David Hackett. *Historians' Fallacies: Toward a Logic of Historical Thought.* New York: Harper & Row, 1970. A ruthless recital of 103 ways to go wrong, illustrated with amusing and sometimes unfair examples, together with sober and constructive suggestions on how to stay clean.

Frankenberg, Celestine G. *Picture Sources.* 2nd ed., New York: Special Libraries Association, 1964. A directory of collections and services including 187 specializing in U.S. history and geography, with a bibliography of finding aids. Out of print. See also Evans, above.

Freidel, Frank, ed. *Harvard Guide to American History.* rev. ed., vols., Cambridge: Harvard University Press, 1974. The standard selective bibliography for books and articles in the field published before 1971. It is usefully organized and thoroughly indexed. The previous edition (Oscar Handlin, ed., 1954) was in one volume and is still good as far as it goes, which is through 1950.

Gregory, Winifred, comp. *American Newspapers, 1821-1936.* New York: H. W. Wilson Co., 1937. Same coverage and arrangement as Brigham but starting with 1821. Locates original files but predates microfilming. To locate filmed newspapers, look in the larger libraries for *Newspapers in Microform: United States, 1948-1972* (Washington, D.C.: Library of Congress, 1973) and any supplements.

Guide to the Study of the United States of America. Prepared under the direction of Roy P. Basler. Washington, D.C.: Library of Congress, 1960; supplement, 1976. These are bargains from the U.S. Superintendent of Documents. Well-annotated and indexed, the first volume contains 6,487 main entries of books published through 1955; the supplement adds 2,943 entries from 1956 through 1965. Good for getting started on obscure special subjects. Available in most middle-sized libraries.

Hale, Richard W., Jr., comp. *Guide to Photocopied Historical Materials in the United States and Canada.* Ithaca: Cornell University Press for the American Historical Association, 1961. Lists 11,137 items from around the world held by 285 institutions. The arrangement of U.S. entries groups types of material (census, county, church, business, personal, etc.) within each state. Gives ownership of positives and negatives as of January 1959.

Hamer, Philip M., ed. *A Guide to Archives and Manuscripts in the United States.* New Haven: Yale University Press, 1961. Brief entries, but about 20,000 of them; arranged by location of collection—state, city, and depository—noting guides to individual collections. Except for archives, its earlier date and smaller size make it a supplement only to the *National Union Catalog. . .*, below.

Hexter, Jack H. *The History Primer.* New York: Basic Books, 1971. Despite the title and the quotation I have used in the text, this is not a simple book. Hexter is a brilliant student of historical explanations who writes with elegance and force, but he writes for the seasoned professional.

Hindle, Brooke. *Technology in Early America: Needs and Opportunities for Study.* Chapel Hill: University of North Carolina Press for the Institute of Early American History and Culture, 1966. Listed here not only for its bibliographical essay, but also for its "Directory of Artifact Collections" by Lucius F. Ellsworth.

Ivins, William M., Jr. *How Prints Look: Photographs With a Commentary.* Boston: Beacon Press, 1958. A paperback by a leading authority, it offers magnified details with explanations.

Mott, Frank Luther. *American Journalism, A History, 1690-1960.* 3rd ed., New York: Macmillan, 1962. A 900-page survey of the newspaper in history. Mott has also written a 5-volume history of American magazines.

National Union Catalog of Manuscript Collections. 11 vols. to date, 1962-70; Washington: Library of Congress Card Division for vols. 3 ff. See these for information on first two volumes. Basic arrangement is by name of collection within each volume of this continuing series, but each entry has its number and the indexes are thorough. Total through 1970 is 25,145 collections in 758 depositories.

Newhall, Beaumont. *The History of Photography From 1839 to The Present Day.* rev. ed., New York: Doubleday, for the Museum of Modern Art, 1972. A handsomely illustrated survey, international in scope, by the former director of the International Museum of Photography (George Eastman House), Rochester, N.Y. See also Taft, below.

Paullin, Charles O. *Atlas of the Historical Geography of the United States.* John K. Wright, ed., Carnegie Institution Publication 401; Washington: Carnegie Institution and American Geographical Society, 1932. A series of historical maps, 1492-1867, followed by specially drawn maps arranged chronologically within topical groups. Few large scale maps. Annotated and indexed. See also Adams' atlas, above, which adds new material.

Poulton, Helen J., and Marguerite S. Howland. *The Historian's Handbook: A Descriptive Guide to Reference Works.* Norman: University of Oklahoma

Press, 1977. Worldwide in scope and selective, it nevertheless has something useful for everyone and is the most recent compilation at present. Available in paperback.

Rath, Frederick L., Jr., and Merrilyn Rogers O'Connell, editors. *Documentation of Collections.* Compiled by Rosemary S. Reese. Nashville: American Association for State and Local History, 1979. This is Vol. 4 of *A Bibliography on Historical Organization Practices.* An annotated guide to expertise on artifacts, decorative arts, fine arts, and folk arts; directed to curators' and collectors' needs, but indispensable for anyone working with materials other than words.

Sealock, Richard B., and Pauline A. Seely. *Bibliography of Place-Name Literature, United States and Canada.* Chicago: American Library Association, 2nd ed., 1967. 3,599 entries, including many gazetteers, arranged by states and annotated. Author and subject indexes.

Spear, Dorothea N. *Bibliography of American Directories through 1860.* Barre, Mass.: Barre Publishers for the American Antiquarian Society, 1961; reprinted 1978 by Greenwood Press. Contains 1,647 entries in one list of cities and states, with locations of libraries known to hold copies of these often scarce sources.

Taft, Robert. *Photography and the American Scene.* New York: Macmillan, 1938; Dover Publications (paper), 1964. A pioneer and still standard work on developments through 1889, this is a social history as well as a review of styles and techniques. Taft was a chemistry professor at the University of Kansas. See also Newhall, above.

United States Local Histories in the Library of Congress; A Bibliography, edited by Marion J. Kaminkow, Baltimore, Md.: Magna Carta Book Company, 1975. 4 vols., and supplement, 1976. It reproduces in book form the shelflist of United States local history in the Library's official catalog. The four volumes deal respectively with: Atlantic States, Maine to New York; Atlantic States, New Jersey to Florida; the Deep South, the Southwest, the Middle West, Alaska, and Hawaii; the West, the Northwest, and the Pacific States. Each region and state is preceded by its LC classification schedule and followed by a supplementary index of places. A select bibliography is provided for each region and state. An expensive set, but its 5,000 pages contain more than 90,000 listings of titles received through mid-1972. The 1976 supplement volume adds titles received through 1975.

Whiffen, Marcus. *American Architecture Since 1780; A Guide to the Styles.* Cambride, Mass.: MIT Press, 1969. A good brief guide for "building watchers" with illustrations, a glossary, and a bibliography. Many more useful *local* guides have also appeared recently, often in paperback editions. And see Blumenson, above.

Wroth, Lawrence. *The Colonial Printer.* Charlottesville: The University Press of Virginia, 1964. Reprint in paperback of the revised 1938 edition of this standard. For later periods, see Clark, above, and Milton W. Hamilton, *The Country Printer* (New York: Columbia University Press, 1936.)

Writing

Ashley, Paul P. *Say It Safely: Legal Limits in Publishing, Radio, and Television*, 5th ed., Seattle: University of Washington Press, 1976. Plagiarism, libel, and infringements on privacy are all entertainingly discussed. See also the titles by Lindey and Wittenberg cited below. All of these, being essentially legal advice, are useful in avoiding trouble, but none is a substitute for a live attorney in dealing with a live issue. Note that on copyright law, this edition of Ashley is not up to date.

Barzun, Jacques, and Henry F. Graff. *The Modern Researcher*, 3rd ed. New York: Harcourt Brace & World, 1979. Part Three of this well-written guide is on writing, including especially good advice on organizing, counsels of perfection on style, and a discussion of translations.

Bernstein, Theodore M. *The Careful Writer: A Modern Guide to English Usage.* New York: Atheneum, 1965; paper ed., 1978. Arranged in alphabetical entries, this is useful for reference and often entertaining to read.

Cantor, Norman F., and Richard I. Schneider. *How to Study History.* New York: Thomas Y. Crowell, 1967. Chapters 8-9 and 11-12 are on organizing and writing historical material including—since this is for college students—book reviews and examinations.

Collison, Robert L. *Indexing Books.* Tuckahoe, N.Y.: John De Graff, 1962; rev. ed., 1972. The most thorough treatment, directed to professionals. For briefer directions, see Kent or the University of Chicago *Manual of Style*, below.

Crawford, Ted. *The Writer's Legal Guide.* New York: Hawthorn Books, 1977. This covers copyrights, contracts, income taxes, and more. Donald F. Johnston, *A Copyright Handbook* (New York: R. R. Bowker Co., 1978), is authoritative and detailed. See also Wittenberg, below.

Follett, Wilson. *Modern American Usage*, A Guide. New York: Hill and Wang, 1966; rev. ed. 1979. This takes up where dictionaries leave off on questions of when a word or phrase is the exact and appropriate one. Edited and completed after Follett's death by Jacques Barzun in collaboration with seven other writers, this relatively new work is not to be confused with an old, standard work from England, H. W. Fowler's *A Dictionary of Modern English Usage*, which stresses British variants.

Finberg, H. P. R., and V. H. T. Skipp. *Local History, Objective and Pursuit.* Newton Abbott, Devon: David Charles, 1967; New York: Augustus M. Kelley, 1967. This may not be the easiest book to locate, but the British experience with local history is a fascinating one as seen through these six very readable essays. Finberg's "How Not to Write a Local History" would amuse and instruct any American historian.

Kent, Sherman. *Writing History.* 2nd ed., Englewood Cliffs, N.J.: Prentice-Hall, 1967 (paper); original ed. 1941. A source of sensible advice as far as this short book goes, with an appendix on "Making an Index" and a model bibliographical essay at the end.

Lindey, Alexander. *Plagiarism and Originality.* New York: Harper, 1952; reprinted, 1974, by Greenwood Press. A lawyer addresses the layman on problems with books, plays, films, art, and music. See also Ashley, above.

Strunk, William, Jr., and E. B. White. *The Elements of Style.* New York, Macmillan, 1959; 3rd ed., 1979. White is a master of the informal essay, and in this 71-page book he has revised and expanded an even briefer text on effective writing done by his professor at Cornell a generation earlier. Strunk had said, in effect, "Do it my way," and with White's endorsement and charm, a great many students of writing have been willing.

University of Chicago Press. *A Manual of Style,* 12th ed., rev., Chicago, 1969. More than a mere guide for this press's editors and authors, the Chicago *Manual* has come to be the most authoritative and complete single reference work of its kind. It emphasizes the formalities, technicalities, and processes of writing, footnoting, editing, and preparing copy for the printer. It advises at length on when to capitalize, hyphenate, or abbreviate a word, but is less concerned with style in the sense of choosing the best word. A glossary and an annotated bibliography are included.

Wittenberg, Philip. *The Protection of Literary Property.* Boston: The Writer, Inc. 1969; rev. ed., 1978. A readable authority on the whole range of copyright, libel, and related legal questions, some of them involving common law rather than statutes. See also note under Ashley, above.

Words Into Type. 3rd ed., rev. Englewood Cliffs, N.J.: Prentice-Hall, Inc., 1974. The newest edition of this reliable old standard for writers and editors. It overlaps the University of Chicago *Manual* (above) but is organized differently and is more helpful on book production planning and on grammar and usage.

Publishing

Alderson, William T., Donna McDonald, and Paula A. Hiles. *A Manual on the Printing of Newsletters.* Nashville: American Association for State and Local History, 1971. Here are 26 sample newsletters arranged roughly in order of quality, with running comments on their costs, materials, and technical and skill requirements. The *Manual* is now out of print; the Association does have a slide/tape training kit, "Newsletter Techniques," for rent.

Appelbaum, Judith, and Nancy Evans. *How to Get Happily Published.* New York: Harper & Row, 1978. Two savvy editors for a large New York firm writing for a wide range of authors. The book's strengths are in its advice on promotion—of author, manuscript, and final product—and its extensive final section, "Resources." On the production process for self-publishers, it is merely breezy.

Arnold, Edmund C. *Ink on Paper 2: A Handbook of the Graphic Arts.* New York: Harper & Row, 1972. A good textbook for home study of all aspects of the art and technology of copy preparation and printing, although other books cover individual topics more adequately.

Dempsey, Hugh A. *How to Prepare a Local History.* Calgary, Alberta, Canada: Glenbow-Alberta Institute, 1969. A modest pamphlet of 21 pages containing some practical advice on promoting community sponsorship and obtaining subscriptions.

Ferguson, Rowena. *Editing the Small Magazine.* 2nd ed. New York: Columbia University Press, 1976. Paperback. A how-to book highly.regarded by those who know how.

Henderson, Bill, ed. *The Publish-It-Yourself Handbook: Literary Tradition and How-To.* Rev. ed. New York: Pushcart Press and Harper & Row, 1980. Paperback. Originally self-published in 1973, this has been revised and marketed by Harper's in paperback. It is not a handbook, but largely a series of personal experiences by contributors, none of them historians. One offers an especially grim view of vanity presses, based on the inside editorial experience. The "how-to" portions are skimpy and casual, but worth attention.

Lee, Marshall. *Bookmaking: The Illustrated Guide to Design and Production.* 2nd ed., rev. New York: R. R. Bowker, 1979. Thorough, thoughtful, and practical—a superlative piece of work, with a guide to sources of information at the end.

Literary Market Place. New York: R. R. Bowker Co., annual. Most libraries have this invaluable registrar of firms and personnal in publishing and allied fields. It includes phone numbers and a buyer's guide. Extensive and current, but not exhaustive. Bowker also publishes the *Publishers Trade List Annual,* a catalog that shows what many publishers are issuing.

Melcher, Daniel, and Nancy Larrick. *Printing and Promotion Handbook,* 3rd ed. New York: McGraw-Hill Book Co., 1966. Comprehensive but a little old now, it is a second choice to Lee, cited above.

Mueller, L. W. *How to Publish Your Own Book.* Detroit: Harlow Press, 1976. Paperback. Mueller writes as a printer whose firm specializes in offering authors a range of services to make self-publishing work. This relatively thorough and always practical guide is itself a major service.

Pocket Pal. 10th Ed., New York, International Paper Co., 1970. A concise handbook on graphic arts production covering most of the same ground as Arnold (above) on technical processes and terms. Frequently revised since 1934, its latest edition is usually quite up to date.

Smith, Cortland Gray. *Editor's Manual.* Cortland Gray Smith, 248 Circle Drive, Plandome, N.Y. 11030, 2nd ed., 1969. Directed to the beginning editor and slanted toward the requirements of journalism, this could serve especially well for newsletter editors as a companion to Alderson, et al., cited above.

White, Jan V. *Editing by Design.* New York: R. R. Bowker, 1974. a large and lively manual focusing on magazine layout but full of ideas and explanations useful to the novice designer of books and newsletters as well.

Writer's Market 1981. Cincinnati: Writer's Digest, 1980. Lists about 500 book publishers and many more magazines, giving addresses, interests, and tips for the freelance writer. New editions appear annually.

Index

162